"If you're like most people, you'd love to slash your grocery bill like the coupon pros you've seen on TV or read about in magazines. But who's got the time-equivalent of a part-time job to pull that off? Prepare to be surprised by how easy it really is to slash your grocery budget by 50 to 70 percent consistently, week after week! In this book Kasey Trenum takes you from start to finish using her uniquely simple strategies. You'll go step-by-step, from collecting coupons to getting organized to understanding store policies and secrets for how to maximize your savings—just like a pro!"

—**Mary Hunt**, personal finance expert and founder of
Debt-Proof Living, author of *7 Money Rules for Life*

"*Couponing for the Rest of Us* will leave your heart and wallet full as you navigate toward prosperity and hope."

—**Amee Cantagallo**, founder of MadameDeals.com

"Finally! Not only does *Couponing for the Rest of Us* walk the reader step-by-tiny-step through the confusing maze of the couponing world, it approaches the process with compassion and grace. Saving money doesn't have to be all about 'me, me, me,' and Kasey inspires us to be better through our good stewardship."

—**Linsey Knerl**, blogger at LilliPunkin.com
and 1099Mom.com

81|15

Couponing

FOR THE **REST OF US**

THE **NOT-SO-EXTREME** GUIDE TO **SAVING MORE**

Kasey Knight Trenum

Revell
a division of Baker Publishing Group
Grand Rapids, Michigan

Published by Revell
a division of Baker Publishing Group
P.O. Box 6287, Grand Rapids, MI 49516–6287
www.revellbooks.com

Printed in the United States of America

Library of Congress Cataloging-in-Publication Data is on file at the Library of Congress, Washington, DC.

ISBN 978-0-8007-2206-7

Unless otherwise indicated, Scripture quotations are from the *Holy Bible*, New Living Translation, copyright © 1996, 2004, 2007 by Tyndale House Foundation. Used by permission of Tyndale House Publishers, Inc., Carol Stream, Illinois 60188. All rights reserved.

Scripture quotations labeled NIV are from the Holy Bible, New International Version®. NIV®. Copyright © 1973, 1978, 1984, 2010 by Biblica, Inc.™ Used by permission of Zondervan. All rights reserved worldwide. www.zondervan.com

Scripture quotations labeled NLV are from the New Life Version, copyright © 1969 by Christian Literature International.

All images courtesy of Cortney Wheeler Photography. Used by permission.

The internet addresses, email addresses, and phone numbers in this book are accurate at the time of publication. They are provided as a resource. Baker Publishing Group does not endorse them or vouch for their content or permanence.

13   14   15   16   17   18   19   7   6   5   4   3   2   1

To my precious daddy, whose life was full of love, generosity, and contagious laughter. A day is coming when I will see you again face-to-face. How thankful I am to have the assurance of your heavenly home. There will never be another like you—your impact on the lives of those around you is beyond what you could have imagined and continues to this day.

To my husband, Gary, and my children, Morgan and Caleb, you are the greatest gifts God could have blessed me with. No one compares to you; I adore you with all that I am.

Most of all, to my heavenly Father, for redeeming my life. Your faithfulness is more than I deserve. Your love for me is astounding and your power to deliver is beyond what I could have ever imagined.

Contents

Contents

About Kasey

It all started with ketchup. When I came out of the grocery store with a bottle of ketchup for 16 cents, the wheels started turning. That was when my world turned upside down. Everything finally came together in a way I had never understood before. The savings kept adding up the more I researched blogs, deals, coupons, and store policies. I had many sleepless nights devouring everything I could possibly find about couponing. If I had discovered all this back in college, I could have saved so much money!

But really, I didn't know exactly what I was doing. As I started purchasing several items each week at a really low price, I began to notice that little by little I no longer needed those products. Unbeknownst to me, I was actually building my pantry. Then I found myself needing to buy only the necessities each week, then only purchasing the items my family used that were really cheap or free. Before I knew it, a couple of months had gone by and I had stocked my pantry with more food than I had ever shopped for without coupons and had paid half the price for it.

My papa always liked to say, "You are always better off when you keep your own money in your pocket." At the time, I just didn't realize how profound that statement would be to me later on in life. The truth is that all these savings from couponing have added up to a part-time job so I don't have to work outside our home. I kept my money in my pocket and spent my time with my children.

I've taken everything I've learned and put it in an easy-to-understand format so everyone can enjoy the benefits of this knowledge without the pressure of it taking too much time. After all, I know how it feels to be stressed with life's responsibilities and burdens, especially the financial ones. With all we have going on, who has the extra time to spend hours a day clipping coupons? I certainly don't, and I'm sure you don't either. I've learned how to balance savings with having a life and without it becoming an obsession. I've never woken up singing the praises of a coupon; I've just sung the joys of saving a ton of money.

But it's not just about the savings. When I started sharing tips with others through the Time 2 $ave workshops, I saw a need in the community. Well, I saw lots of needs. I saw families who were broke or were going through an illness. I saw elderly people who needed help with their groceries. I saw single mothers who couldn't afford diapers. I saw people who lost all they had because of a tornado, flood, or hurricane. I started looking outward and helping others through the money I was saving and the deals I was getting. I haven't stopped since.

I'm not just about getting more for less; I'm about making a difference.

What Others Are Saying (and Saving!)

From college students to entrepreneurs to single, working, or stay-at-home moms, everyone who has used my philosophy has a reason for being super excited about their savings. Read on!

Time 2 $ave

Thanks for teaching me these techniques. I have loved it and we love the donation box that we have set aside for The Ronald McDonald House. . . . I'm a single mom and love to help others, but never had the means to do it until now. It's awesome and the kids have really gotten into it with me.—Sandy

I have just finished a back-to-school and a grocery shopping trip using your tips. I saved over $200! Also, our pantry and two freezers are beginning to fill up! Everyone in our household is thrilled!—Tiffany

My sister, daughter, and I took your class around the first of this year, and were soon contacted by our local newspaper that was doing a story on saving money. My daughter and I commented about our class experience and how much money we saved. My sister and I live next door to each other, so we grocery shop together. Saving money has become a contest for us! Sometimes she wins, sometimes I win, but we are both saving tons of money. I have not had this many groceries in my married life! Which is twenty-five years! Thanks for the help!—Tammy

I am stopped every day in the stores and asked how I do coupons. I've been shopping with them for at least twenty-five years. I save several hundred dollars every couple of days. Most of the food and other items I donate. It's the rush of the savings that I enjoy since all my children are grown. My daughter and grandchildren get a lot of benefit from my shopping. Time 2 $ave has been an added blessing to my shopping experiences.—Dawn

I attended your workshop in South Pittsburgh and I really learned a lot. I have more than made back the $40 for the workshop, and I am using most of my stockpile to make Christmas baskets for my family. I have also shared the coupon savings with friends at church and my family in other states. Thank you so much for doing these workshops and keeping us updated each day of how to "wheel and deal." I love it.—Nora

Before we were married, my husband and I decided to live on one income so I could be at home with any children we might have. The Lord has blessed us with two kids and I have been able to be home with them since birth. But financially this is not always easy. . . . It has been five weeks since I took your first class and my grocery budget has gone down from $95 to $75 per week. My goal is $45 per week. . . . I regularly save 50 percent or more on my stockpile items. . . . My best shopping trip to date was to Publix. I spent $4.17 and saved $28.36. My husband was with me and when he saw the total, he was amazed. . . . The next day at Publix (a new sale week), I spent $7, saved $21—on fourteen items. . . . I can't thank you all enough for your ministry.—Elizabeth

My grocery bill and budget has been $500 a month and we are building a house. I was trying to cut our bills down. The first time I went shopping, I was blown away how coupons changed my life. I went to the grocery store, bought $124 worth of groceries, and paid only $44. WOW!—Sharvetta

Time 2 Give

I've used coupons off and on for years. A friend at work told me about your blog in February and now I've turned into a coupon fanatic. Until reading your postings on your blog, I never realized stores doubled coupons or that you could "stack" coupons. Now, for the first time, my family has "name-brand" foods and plenty more. This past week I was able to donate a bounty of toiletry items for a Wounded Warriors project. What a blessing!—Betty

Although we're considered "seniors," saving money is still as important, especially since we're on a limited income. After taking the coupon classes, I changed my way of shopping to incorporate what I had learned. The money we save now allows us to enjoy some of the benefits of being retired, like camping trips, extended vacations, and taking more trips for mission work. We can now spend time volunteering and giving to others in ways we wouldn't have if we hadn't been challenged to live focused outwards. Being able to bless others with groceries is a great way to be an example of Christ to them. I recommend the classes for anyone wanting to save money, shop wisely, and be able to share more with others.—Johnnie

I took the class last fall in Dayton, Tennessee. I am amazed at the amount of products I have stockpiled, so many that I give to others on a regular basis. I praise God for allowing me to minister this way. There are three elderly couples in my church who enjoy the fruits of my abundance. To hear them say those groceries and other household items are an answer to prayer fills my heart with joy. The soup kitchen, my family, and friends also receive overflows. I especially enjoyed saving on VistaPrint's free business cards. I ordered 500 at a great price and used them for the Great Strides Walk for Cystic Fibrosis. They were a great hit! The best thing is I am staying in my budget.—Kathy

Acknowledgments

It's true; God chooses the weak things of this world to confound the wise. I am the most unlikely girl to have been chosen for this journey. The timing of this call on my life—the worst possible—my ability to walk this calling out on my own—zero. Without him, I would have never taken the first step. With him, I have been redeemed and have experienced the joy of being carried by one stronger than me. He is my Healer, my Father, my Provider, and the Source of my joy. He picked me up out of the miry clay and set my foot upon a rock.

To my husband Gary, thank you for your love and support. I could never have finished this project without your help. You stepped in and cooked, cleaned, took care of our children, and anything else I needed so that I could meet my deadlines. The season of our life that led up to this crazy world of couponing was at times more than either of us thought we could bear. It felt like the desert would never end, and that we'd always be in the valley. I'm so thankful that God is true to his Word, as we see his promises manifesting in our life. There is no one else I'd want to be on this journey with. I love you . . . forever. You are my rock, and a mighty man of God.

To my precious babies, Morgan and Caleb, I'm so thankful that God chose me to be your mommy. Your heart to serve Jesus, give to others, and desire to walk in the calling that God has for you is more than I could ask. Thank you for your patience during this process and being Mommy's biggest cheerleaders. Morgan, your light shines brightly in everything you put your hands to. Since you were a tiny little girl, your faith in Jesus and the depth of your love for him has been an inspiration. You are impacting the kingdom, baby girl. Don't ever stop or let the things of this world hold you back from your calling. You are anointed beyond your years. Caleb, my prayer warrior, how I love to hear your sweet voice come before the throne of glory. Your sincere, faith-filled prayers have already moved mountains. That Christmas morning when we found out that we were expecting you was a fulfillment of God's promise over your life and his faithfulness to our family. Your prayers are powerful, your calling is mighty.

To my daddy, there are no words that describe how much I miss you. You never sat me down and taught me how to give; I learned by watching your life. You lived an honorable life full of love for your family and generosity to others. I love you more than words can say, and will always be a daddy's girl.

For my mom, who taught me the importance of prayer and fasting. Because of you, we were in church every time the doors were open. I'm so glad that you never gave up praying for Daddy's salvation. Through your perseverance I learned the power of prayer.

Blake, I have adored you since the day Mamma and Daddy brought you home from the hospital. I see in you the same kind of tender, giving heart as Daddy's. He would have been so proud of the man you have become.

To Gary and Mary Trenum, your prayers mean the world. Thank you for your love and support.

To Joan Tankersley, my mentor, friend, encourager, PR/creative director, and business coach. Your imprint on my life is immeasurable.

To my literary agent, Esther Fedorkevich, thank you for believing in me, sticking with me through the process, and tirelessly pitching this book. You are nothing short of amazing.

To A. J. Gregory, my Jersey girl, I am forever grateful for your relentless dedication to getting this project off the ground. You are an amazing friend and writer.

Andrea Doering at Revell, I love how you took the message of couponing I shared with you home to your family. Your personal experience was instrumental in bringing this book to life.

Carrie Woods, you are a fearless writer who flat-out knows how to whip out words and meet deadlines. I'm forever grateful to you.

Jamie Miles, your input in this book was invaluable. Your daily contribution and dedication to Time 2 $ave is more than I could ask for. It's been a crazy ride, sweet friend; I'm so thankful to have you on this journey.

Lindsay Davis, Twila Bennett, and Robin Barnett, y'all are amazing. Your insight, wisdom, and experience are invaluable to this project.

Dr. Jonathon Kerley, thank you for your obedience to God. You impacted my life for the kingdom and changed the course of my story. Thank you.

Kristin Kerley, how thankful I am for your friendship and kindred spirit. Your wisdom and heart as a mother always remind me to keep my eyes on Jesus and what he has called me to as a wife and mom. I treasure your support and prayers!

Duane and Candace Goff, from our first dinner meeting you challenged me to dream big. Who would have thought that those big dreams would one day come true? Your words of wisdom, business insight, prayers, and encouragement have been priceless.

To Debby McCuiston, thank you for your servant's heart. You have been a lifeline, prayer warrior, friend, and confidant. Thank you for sowing so selflessly into my life. You have truly loved me to Jesus.

To Sharon Maloney, the greatest listener I know. Your patience, love, and wisdom nurtured my heart during the darkest hours of my journey.

Pastor Hubert Seals, your dedication to our family is beyond anything we could have asked. You and Cathy have walked beside us through every valley. Thank you for your love, prayers, and endless support.

To all the girls that make up the Time 2 $ave team: Jamie, Rachel, Lindsay, Chantal, and Rosie, I couldn't do it without you. Your contribution makes a difference in the lives of so many people. Rosie and Rachel, you went from being the best co-workers anyone could ask for to part of my team. I am so blessed to have friends like you.

To Kelly Thompson, who helped co-found Time 2 $ave.

To every blog reader, without you Time 2 $ave would have been only an idea. Every time you share a post with a friend, forward a deal to a loved one, invite someone to our Facebook community, share a coupon at the store, or give from your heart, I am forever thankful.

Introduction

Thirty-one-year-old Jay has a nickname that some men might find embarrassing. His friends call him "the Coupon Lady." It doesn't bother him, though. In fact, he likes it. Especially because while he is definitely not a lady, he *is* a coupon guru. Skeptical at first, the Coupon Lady couldn't imagine spending hours dissecting a newspaper to save a couple bucks. But what he learned changed his life. He doesn't chat with his buddies anymore about fantasy football leagues or NASCAR races; he talks to them about how much he saves on groceries.

Jayne, a woman who has learned to fit couponing into her life and is thriving because of it, was exasperated when I first met her. She has three kids under the age of ten, works a full-time job, cares for her ill mother in her home, and tries to maintain her sanity in the midst of it all (not an easy thing to do most days). "I can barely get my head above water," she told me as she let out a big sigh. "The last thing I want to do is spend all night researching the best coupons."

I simply nodded and thought, "Believe me, neither do I."

Jayne took a deep breath and continued, "If I have to sacrifice more time just to save a few bucks, I've got to be honest. It's not worth it. You can keep your coupons."

Oh Jayne, I so get it.

You've seen the TV shows. You've heard about how much your friends, folks at the grocery store, or your frugal neighbor saves through these valuable pieces of paper. Heck, you might have even tried couponing before. But chances are, you weren't successful (otherwise you wouldn't be reading this book). And chances are, there is a small (maybe even a teensy-weensy) part of you that doubts couponing will really help you to save big.

When I started couponing I faced many doubts, questions, and concerns, some of which you may have. I want to start by addressing and dispelling some of the myths I've heard that say couponing won't work. Misconceptions such as: "I don't have the time." "There's never any coupons for things I normally buy." "I like to stick with certain brands." "If it works so well, why isn't everyone doing it?"

So before we get into the nitty-gritty of couponing, let's take some time to address the questions I get asked the most (and the ones you just might be thinking). Because I get it, I am not a crazy coupon lady. I'm just a regular stay-at-home working mom who is trying to save some money and some time.

Questions & Answers

Q. I already have too much on my plate and couponing looks like a part-time job. I don't have time to do this!

A. I get how hectic life can be for the average person, especially for working mothers. I know because I am one. Balancing a family, health, life stresses, daily responsibilities, social commitments, work, and [you fill in the blank] is not an easy task. It's an art form where you learn (and sometimes relearn) what priorities are important.

On a personal note, I hear your pain. If anyone thought she didn't have time to coupon, it was me. I didn't even consider it as a remote possibility. When I was regularly visiting my father who was battling cancer and dealing with the prospect of losing him to the disease, the last thing on my mind was saving money and grocery shopping. It was a race I couldn't win; I didn't even want to try. I felt I needed to savor every visit with my dad and the time I had left with him, not spend time seeing what corners I could cut in my budget.

There are seasons in our lives when we won't have time to coupon because we are dealing with a traumatic life experience, whether a divorce, loss of a loved one, marital problems, or job stress. During these times, it's okay not to worry about saving every last penny. Your mind is concerned with more important matters.

The reality of life without my dad had barely begun to sink in when the company my husband worked for had a merger and decided to eliminate his entire division. Did I happen to mention it was the day after my father's funeral? I didn't understand why God had allowed so many difficult things to happen in my life at the same time. Spiritually, emotionally, and physically I was depleted. Even so, at this point we were forced to face the reality that we could no longer live the same lifestyle as we always had. It was time to stop spending and find ways to save.

I had to change some habits. For instance, when we were completely out of necessities like diapers, toilet paper, and Diet Coke, I would make a mad dash to the store. This usually happened late at night because that's when life slowed down enough for me to realize my son had to have diapers, I wasn't willing to go back to the old "magazine" toilet paper that my great-grandparents used in their outhouse, and I flat out loved and needed my Diet Coke.

This worked for a while, but I soon discovered it wasn't enough. Time or no time, I couldn't afford not to use couponing as an avenue to save. Soon I began to see how the benefits outweighed my investment. It was worth it to have several hundred dollars a month back in our budget, especially when our other household expenses weren't going down. It was worth it to have an abundance of groceries at home. It was worth it not to make emergency runs to the store at midnight for diapers, toilet paper, and Diet Coke.

I've often asked workshop participants, "If I gave you a hundred bucks to jump in the car with us and go for an hour ride, would you do it?" The answer is always an overwhelming, "Um, HELLO! Yes! Of course, yes!" Would you? Will couponing take some of your time? Yes, but not much. I'll show you the ropes so you can save both time and money.

Q. **I have a small family. There's just one (or two) of us. I don't see how using coupons could help us much since our grocery bill isn't that high.**

A. The size of your family doesn't matter. Whatever your grocery bill is, there is usually room to save. Even if you only spend $50 a week, wouldn't you like to cut that down to $20 or $30? Aside from the numbers, when you shop ahead of time to buy what you use, it takes the stress of *having* to go to the grocery store out of your life.

Couponing for the Rest of Us isn't just a how-to book on saving money. Each chapter is filled with real-life stories of men, women, and families who have made a difference in someone else's life through following the Time 2 $ave philosophy, as well as stories of people who have been touched by the generous giving of those in our community.

Q. **This seems like a lot of work and I'm not an organized person. I don't think I can keep up with all this!**

A. Oh my! If you look up "unorganized" in the dictionary, you'll find my picture. Oh, wait. Never mind. You won't. I didn't make it to get my picture taken because I couldn't find my car keys. As a creative person, my thoughts are all over the place, my mind never stops racing, and I literally lose my cell phone and keys every single day. I really (really!) want to be organized and I have tried to help myself in this area more ways than I can count. But you know what? I was not created that way.

You can imagine my struggle with organizing my coupons. I had to find a way that worked for me (and didn't consume my life) and that I could stick with for the long haul. I don't have to compare myself to other people who are super organized and even alphabetize their coupons. If I put that expectation on myself, it's a big fat accident waiting to happen. Remember, couponing isn't all-or-nothing. It's what fits into whatever season of life you are in right now. What works for one person might not work for another; we are all unique. Be patient as you figure out what makes sense and works best for you.

Q. **I've seen where couponing revolves around stockpiling and having massive amounts of food in your house. I don't think I can (or want) to go there.**

A. Fabulous! That makes two of us. My goal is to teach you how to save your family money and open up doors to give. It's all about simplicity here; couponing isn't an all-or-nothing deal. Couponing success isn't measured by the size of your stockpile. I'd much rather be known for giving.

Q. My friend uses coupons and now she won't buy anything without one. I think she's too obsessive about it, and I really don't want to add that kind of stress or pressure to my life.

A. At first, I felt the same way. It took me some time to realize that the unnecessary expectations I was putting on myself were adding stress to my life. It wasn't worth it then, and it's not worth it now. It's okay to purchase an item without a coupon, it's okay to pay full price, and it's okay to miss a deal. After all, there is more to life than coupons. Of course my goal is to use coupons and not pay full price. However, if it means sacrificing family time, a date night, sanity, or anything else, I've learned to release that pressure.

Q. I would like to give more to my community and help others who are in need. How can I do that when I'm struggling to pay my own bills?

A. Coupons can change your family's finances and give you the tools to invest in the lives of others in ways you never dreamed possible without your financial situation changing. Sounds good, huh? It's not too good to be true. Balance is the key. You'll have the tools to save money *and* be equipped to give. It's up to you to make it real in your life.

Q. How will my family be affected? I'm not sure they are on board for shopping with coupons.

A. My family went through many transitions that related to using coupons and being more intentional in our saving and spending. Although couponing appeared to be the driving force for change, it really was just a tool. I learned powerful heart lessons during this process that I'll explain in more detail in chapter 10.

Here's the thing. My kids are not thrilled about cutting coupons. Like me, my daughter has ADHD and when it comes to clipping pieces of paper, her attention span is pretty limited. But this doesn't mean my family wasn't influenced in a positive way by this new means of saving. They learned that just because they ask Mommy to buy them Teddy Grahams doesn't mean that I'm going to buy them. Now they ask, "When you get a coupon for Teddy Grahams, can you buy them, Mom? Please?" (Of course I will.) My little ones have finally learned what delayed gratification looks like.

Most of all, I've noticed so many opportunities that have opened in our family as a result of couponing. It isn't just about cutting out a piece of paper and handing it over to a cashier. We eat together around the dinner table more. My kids help with preparing our meals. And we've become more intentional in our giving. Yes, all of this has happened as a result of coupons.

Q. What do the stores think about shoppers using tons of coupons? Do they dread seeing you coming?

A. I've learned that how a store reacts to me depends on how I treat the store, the staff, and other shoppers. If I'm in line with a buggy full of groceries and my hands full of coupons, I always look behind me and encourage those who have a few items to go in front of me. I can't count how many times I've heard people whisper or say behind my back, "Oh great, I'm behind one of those 'couponers' who hold up the line with all their coupons." I can politely and honestly say that I don't; I am not one of those kinds of couponers.

It goes back to my foundational belief system to treat others as I would want to be treated. Since I have heard complaints from people who have had bad experiences with couponers, it has opened my eyes to strengthen relationships with grocery store managers and their staff. On occasion I try to bring the staff an extra set of coupons so they too can get the deals. So no, stores definitely don't dread seeing me come in. Many times I even get a hug from those who work there and recognize me.

Q. All I've ever found coupons for is junk food. Can I use coupons when I eat a natural or organic diet?

A. I get asked this question all the time and understand the desire to feed your family healthy foods. I could never afford to purchase organic foods before I started couponing. If you only used coupons to purchase your household products and personal items you could still make a substantial cut in your grocery spending. However, I have found that I purchase more organic and natural foods with couponing than I did before. Since we understand that eating healthy is a priority for our Time 2 $ave community, we keep our eyes open for organic coupons and deals. We have a coupon database that makes finding coupons for organic items a breeze. You can even search for coupons by a specific brand or type of food. We'll talk more about the coupon database in chapter 6.

Q. I've always thought people who use coupons end up purchasing things they don't need just because they have a coupon for it.

A. Guilty! I did it. Most people do, especially in the beginning. However, you'll soon figure out the items that your family uses and what items make good donations. Beyond that, I'll save you some time here. If you can't donate it, even if it's free or cheap, it's not worth it. In some states you will still have to pay tax on the full purchase price before coupons. My mission has been to simplify; if my family doesn't use it and I can't donate it, then it's just going to take up space in my home. You can always share your coupons with friends, schools, military programs, and so forth.

Q. Can't I get the store generic brand cheaper than using coupons?

A. I used to purchase almost everything generic. Once I started couponing that changed! There are rarely coupons available for generic items. If I purchase a name-brand item when it's on sale combined with a coupon, the savings is much greater than generics. In the rare case that a generic product is cheaper, I have no problem buying the generic. It's not that I am endorsing brand-name products over generic products. Instead, my goal is saving money.

Q. I've never been good at math—I can't do this. It seems like there's a lot of adding, doubling, and subtracting involved.

A. Don't worry, I was never good at math and you don't have to be either. Besides, who said you can't use a calculator? Throw one in your purse or use your smartphone. On the other hand, while I never set out to sharpen my math skills, as time has gone by I've gotten pretty good at doing math in my head. I prefer a calculator, but if I don't have one handy it's okay.

Q. How many grocery stores do you shop each week?

A. Lately I am happy to make it to one. I have been asked this question more times than I can count. It is not necessary to shop more than one store, or even to shop every single week for that matter. Whether you save 5 percent or 70 percent, you are still saving. Couponing has to fit into your life, not become your life.

Q. I have a membership to a private warehouse club for shopping in bulk. Don't you think I get better prices there?

A. Most of the time warehouse stores do not accept coupons. My goal is to purchase the items that our family uses at the lowest possible price. The real savings comes in when I am able to use a coupon on an item that is already discounted. Buying in large quantities or bulk limits the number of coupons you can use. For example, if I am purchasing Progresso soup I want to use a coupon on each can to get the cheapest price. A warehouse club doesn't give me that option. I think it's a great place to go for a snack (yummy samples) but not to cut my grocery bill.

Q. Who's this book for?

A. Wanna save some money and maintain balance? This book is for you. Basically, if you eat and use household and personal care products this book will teach you how to save money. It doesn't matter if you're a single mom, a family of four, a college student, or a bachelor. Couponing can make a financial difference.

So guess what? It's time to dive into learning about how this whole thing works. All the ins and outs, all the little secrets I have learned and put to good use over the last few years. We will look at tools you can use to truly make a lasting difference in your budget, we will learn about the basics (and the not-so basics!), and we will all agree to understand that couponing shouldn't take over your life. Your time with your children and with your family is the most important thing. I just want to help make it all come together a little easier for you. Believe it or not, shopping can be fun, and I'm going to show you how!

1

More Than Just Coupons

Those who sow with tears will reap with songs of joy.
Psalm 126:5 NIV

I don't like coupons.

Before you throw this book across the room and wonder why I'm writing about couponing, hear me out.

No, I don't like couponing. I don't dream about it. I don't salivate over newspaper inserts. I don't hoot and holler when I find a rare coupon. But what I *do* get excited about is what I get with couponing—a ton of savings! I remember the first time I saved $12.37. I hollered so loud leaving the store you could have heard me in China.

I started couponing out of necessity, not because I loved it. The company my husband worked for merged with another and his division was eliminated. So my husband lost his job, we couldn't keep up with our mortgage payments, and our bills kept piling up. You might be in the same boat. Maybe the current state of the economy has affected your household and your one-income family has gone to no-income. Maybe you have less and less money to spend each week, and even after budgeting, you still have little to use for necessities like food and household items. Maybe you are skeptical about the amount of savings you can really see with coupons, or you doubt there are ways to save on the special kind of food you typically buy. No matter what situation you are in or how you feel about coupons, I'm here to share from personal experience that couponing works. And it can do wonders for other parts of your life besides finances.

I don't get fired up only because of how much our family saves; I also get excited about what couponing does for me outside my family. As I was writing this, tornadoes devastated much of the town where I live in Tennessee. I was able to take several packs of diapers to the Red Cross since I had been purchasing them on sale and with a coupon for the purpose of giving. Also, since I regularly buy products to donate, I had boxes of stuff—razors, deodorant, toothpaste, and canned goods—to contribute to families who lost everything in that disaster.

Early Lessons

Couponing was something I had tried previously, but it didn't work for several reasons. I would invest time clipping coupons with the best of intentions and then forget to take them to the store. When I did happen to remember to bring them with me, one of two things would happen: I would forget to give them to the cashier at checkout, or my coupons saved me a whopping fifty cents. Not only that, I was also the most non-couponing person you could find. All the numbers associated with prices, sales, deals—blah, blah, blah—they stressed me out. I hated keeping lists. I hated keeping budget spreadsheets. And I never scoured for sales.

I didn't learn about extreme budgeting from my parents, though they did teach me about work ethic and financial discipline. My parents were frugal in that they would tell me we couldn't afford this or that or we simply didn't need certain things. I saw them—particularly my mother—exert a lot of self-control when it came to making purchases. This discipline helped lay a foundation for how I viewed finances. I had my first job at fifteen, and I enjoyed the independence of not having to ask my parents for money. Not long after, I got a second job. The following year I squeezed in job number three.

My parents also talked a lot about saving money, and they always encouraged me to save when I started earning my own money. Mom and Dad were purposeful in letting me know that although some of my friends had really nice things that I would have liked, the reality was that we couldn't afford those same things. Although I'm sure many of my friends' parents could afford to buy just about anything, I know some of them made great sacrifices to give their kids whatever they wanted, even to the detriment of their own finances. I am so thankful that instead of finding a way to give me everything I wanted, my parents chose to give me a gift that is priceless—financial wisdom.

I learned that the world doesn't revolve around me and that "things" come with a cost. It's not necessarily the price tag hanging from whatever item is the cutest, newest, or coolest; it's how much that item will cost me in the long run. My parents didn't believe in going into debt for anything unnecessary. They showed me how to save for what I wanted, not charge it and spend years paying it off. Through their wisdom, I learned how to be content with what I had.

Like your typical college kid, however, I temporarily forgot those great lessons my parents taught me about price and cost, and I ended up accumulating a few thousand dollars of credit card debt. When I started my freshman year, I jumped headfirst into my first credit card offer. I didn't stop there. Anytime I went to the store and the cashier offered me 10 percent off my purchase if I signed up for a credit card, I was lured in like a kid in a candy shop. How could I say no? It was an exciting time in my life because I had independence, especially financial independence. With those plastic demons, I bought all the clothes I wanted and bought my friends whatever they wanted.

Nine months later, the bills from my out-of-control spending habits finally caught up with me. I was way over my head and my expenses outweighed the money I was bringing in. This was the one and only time that my parents rescued me. I learned never to make that same mistake again. Credit cards are not free money.

Another life lesson that has stuck with me is the importance of honesty and integrity. After I had my first checking account for a while, I made a big boo-boo. I bounced a check. I came home from school one day and my daddy handed me the yellow postcard from the bank stating my error. He warned that all I had in life was my name and reputation and proceeded to tell me, "If I go to this bank and ask to borrow one million dollars, they're going to give it to me because they know me and they know I'm going to tell the truth and pay them back." The next day, Daddy took me to the bank to deposit money into my account to correct my mistake. And he stood by my side while I, with much embarrassment, apologized to the bank officer for spending money I didn't have.

The most precious lesson I carry with me every day is the legacy of giving that my daddy lived. Though the goal at Time 2 $ave is teaching people to live a lifestyle of giving, it didn't become a goal of mine by chance. I saw it in action through my dad. I can't count the number of times he would stop at our pastor's home and drop off fresh vegetables from my grandfather's garden along with a ham he had purchased at the grocery store. Daddy anonymously left these groceries at the back door, never seeking recognition or credit. That's the kind of man he was. Time and time again, I saw my daddy giving away food or money to people who were struggling. His heart was tender to the needs of others.

Ironically, Daddy knew about stockpiling long before I did. He loved buying groceries and multiple cans of tomatoes, barbeque sauce, ketchup, and other condiments when he found a great deal. He would open his kitchen cabinets and show me with great pride all he had bought and what a great deal he had gotten. Like father, like daughter.

My daddy got really excited when he saved some money. My mom recently told me that years ago they had invited her boss and his wife over for dinner along with another couple. While the women were putting the finishing touches on dinner, my daddy started telling the guys about this great price on a ham he had gotten at Quality. The store was actually called Quality Grocery Store, but my daddy just called it Quality in his long, Southern drawl. The next thing you know, right before my mom was about to put dinner on the table, she noticed the men getting ready to leave. Guess where they were going? To Quality to get themselves a good deal on ham. My mom was so embarrassed.

Though I understood the importance of being frugal, the world of strict budgeting didn't resonate with me. I wasn't into price comparisons of different stores. I thought it was irrelevant. If I was out of milk, I needed to buy milk. And I could buy either the cheap one or the expensive one. That was it, end of story. If milk cost five bucks one week and three the next, it didn't matter to me.

I also didn't get too excited at great deals on groceries or household supplies. I have to admit, I still don't. Here's a little secret—it's okay if you don't either. You can enjoy couponing and saving money without going bananas. (Now shopping for clothes is an entirely different story. I get crazy excited about my favorite store's new fall line or a great online promo code!) Buying common necessities like milk, gas, and food was something I had to do, so why even bother looking for a great sale?

When the Walls Closed In

Things changed when the reality of our financial situation set in. The housing bubble burst and my husband, Gary, and I were left with two spec houses that didn't sell for two years. So including the house we lived in, we had three mortgages. During that time, we hadn't changed our lifestyle or spending habits, fully expecting the housing market to bounce right back. But when we realized that real estate was only getting worse, we had to look at cutting back our spending.

Within that period, my father was diagnosed with incurable brain cancer. Over the course of the next ten months, my family frequently made the three-hour trip to visit him, which meant additional expenses in gas, food, and so forth. My dad's diagnosis was so devastating, I couldn't even think about our financial situation.

If that wasn't enough, the day after my daddy's funeral, Gary's position at his company was eliminated due to a merger. Thankfully, we had made good financial decisions up to that point. We took budgeting seminars and didn't have any debt other than our homes. But the more I dipped into our savings, the more I knew we had to find a real way to save money.

These difficult and devastating situations that hit one after another like ocean waves changed me. Each time I got knocked off my feet, another layer of my life was torn away. Nothing material in this world mattered to me anymore. It didn't matter if we lost all three houses. I just wanted to be with my dad and spend as much time with him and the rest of my family as I could. For the first time I understood how fragile life is and how the impact of one moment can change everything.

I see now that I was a proud young woman and had to be humbled before God could use me. Although I may have accomplished great career goals, accumulated material possessions that I thought were important, and saved money along the way, all of those things were truly meaningless. It's the message found in Ecclesiastes 2:11, "When I surveyed all that my hands had done and what I had toiled to achieve, everything was meaningless, a chasing after the wind; nothing was gained under the sun" (NIV).

I didn't realize it then but the painful pruning that was taking place was for my own good. Without all that was going on, I'm not sure I would have ever turned to couponing. I probably would have kept my head in the sand and lived as if our financial situation had not changed. I am thankful that God chose to use coupons to show me how big he is and how small my circumstances really are in his eyes. And that no matter how messed up I am or how incapable I perceive myself to be, he only sees what he can do through me.

God also taught me about the kindness of others, which is one reason I am so passionate about giving. After my daddy's funeral, our church family blew us away with their generosity. Almost every day we received gift cards or money in the mail from these sweet people. I had never been on this side of giving before. You see, I always gave to others from the time I first started earning my own money. This time God allowed me to feel his arms wrap around us through the love of other people. There were many people we knew who could not afford what they gave us, but they sacrificed nonetheless. I experienced God meeting my needs, and I had to lay aside my pride and allow people to love on me, support me, and give to us.

At this juncture in my life, couponing was not remotely on my radar. Grocery shopping was just a necessity; I had no idea that the option of lowering my grocery bill even existed. I had no idea about sales cycles. Occasionally I would price match, but not that often; I had to be pretty desperate. My plan was always the same. I'd go to the grocery store, buy what I needed, and discover the same thing every time. Whether I had seven items or thirty items, my bill was always $150 to $200. I used to joke that the cash register was preprogrammed because my total never changed.

I remember when I found out about a particular deal at a local grocery store. (Keep in mind that I had lived within a few minutes of this store since 1996, but I never knew about these deals.) Baby wipes were free with a store coupon and you could also get two free jars of baby food. What? Where had I been all this time? When I pulled up to the store, I wondered why the parking lot wasn't full. Where was everyone?

I was blown away by the feeling of walking out of the store with free baby wipes and two jars of brand-name baby food. The fact that I could do this every day if I wanted to was nuts. Why wasn't everyone else taking advantage of this great deal? I couldn't help but think of all the people who could benefit from free baby stuff, from single mothers with infants to people who could donate the items to moms in need.

Even though the baby wipe deal was incredible, it didn't help the rest of my grocery bill. I remember the week I needed ketchup. When you're broke, condiments are no longer a necessity; they become a luxury. Besides, with all the Happy Meals our kids ate, I knew there had to be ketchup somewhere in our car. If I cleaned it out and found some little, shiny packets, surely I could buy some time.

Right before finding the ketchup deal that turned my world upside down, I found photos online of women who had taken pictures of their groceries. Not only did they take pictures, they also stacked their purchases in neat piles on their kitchen counters and made them look pretty. I thought, *Who are these people? Who has time to make groceries look beautiful? I can barely keep all our clothes washed, never mind decorate my kitchen counter with a neat stack of groceries to photograph.* But I'll be honest, I was intrigued. I couldn't help staring at those photos. It's like seeing something gross; you can't help looking at it, as much as you don't want to. When I discovered how much these women had paid for their groceries—well, it's no wonder they took pictures of them. I would too! I wanted to save like them. I wanted to find these great deals. I wanted my own groceries I could take pictures of.

Turning Point

That same week I found out I could get brand-name ketchup for $0.16 when I combined the store sale price with a manufacturer coupon. I couldn't believe it. The only thing I had ever bought for 16 cents was chewing gum. I was beside myself and didn't believe it would work. But it did. When I was in line checking out, I thought the store would be mad at me. But nobody was upset. In fact, the cashiers waved as I left. They must not have been paying attention. For the next few days, I took trips to the store to get more ketchup. I didn't realize it at the time, but I was building my pantry (even if it was only with ketchup).

I thought ketchup would be the last amazing deal I'd ever get, but the trend continued each week with different items. The next week it was salsa. I made several trips to get the $0.36 jar of salsa, all the while adding to my pantry. I remember thinking that there must be a disgruntled employee in corporate who was going to get fired, then no more super cheap groceries. Why didn't other people know about these kinds of savings? Why weren't they following me out to my car? Funny I thought that, because within a few months people *were* following me to my car to find out how I got my groceries for next to nothing.

Soon I discovered another grocery store that doubled coupons every day. The store had been there forever, but I never knew about their couponing policy. From that point on, couponing became trial and error. By that time my husband had gotten another job and had to go out of town for two weeks for training. I don't think I slept while he was away because I was up every night reading about couponing. I wanted to learn how to do this thing. I wanted to know how to maximize my savings. But it was tough. I felt like I was learning a new language. No one I knew shopped like this. I'd heard of it from seeing the couponing ladies on TV, but I didn't learn much from watching them because they never showed me *how* to do it.

After a while, when I started going to the store for my regular grocery trips to get necessities, I realized I didn't need much. For instance, I didn't need to buy ketchup anymore. Or salsa, spaghetti sauce, laundry detergent, or pasta. It's because for weeks I had stocked up on three or four items at a time. I was so caught up in saving a ton of money, I didn't have any idea I was beginning to build my pantry and shop in an entirely different way. The best part was, my grocery bill started to dwindle. As I continued to stock up on a couple of items each week at a super cheap price, our grocery bill continued to drop until we were only paying $30 to $40 a week. That's a huge difference from the $150 to $200 we had been spending.

Before I knew it, cashiers and shoppers at the stores would ask me how I could buy so much for so little. I couldn't stand knowing people were paying full price if they were in need, and I wanted to help them. The impact on my family's financial situation was so unbelievable, even with three mortgages, I couldn't help but share my "secrets" with whoever asked.

All about Balance

After spending hours and hours researching deals and grocery stores, I had to come to a place where I had more balance. Even things we do with the best of intentions can get out of hand. I remember feeling anxious and struggling with not going to the drugstore each week to get the freebies that I knew other people needed. Contact solution, for example. One bottle of the stuff is about eight bucks. That's pretty expensive. When contact solution was completely free, I felt guilty if I didn't make it to the drugstore that week.

While being able to give is a gift, it comes without condemnation. Instead of continuing to feel guilty because of deals that I would inevitably miss at grocery stores, I began to teach others about those savings. Those people were then inspired to help others, whether through teaching or giving, and together we made (and continue to make) a greater impact on the community as a whole. It's a beautiful cycle.

I do have to admit, however, there were times that it was hard to pay full price for something I knew would probably be really cheap or free the following week. In fact, one night I had a friend over. We were eating pizza and I realized I was out of paper towels and napkins. I hadn't gotten any because they weren't on sale that week. I whipped out a roll of toilet paper and told my friend, "Here. This is your napkin." This particular friend is a germaphobe so I was messing with her a little bit. She was very gracious and laughed about it, but in that moment I realized something. Not everyone is going to be okay with using toilet paper as a napkin, even if it's fresh out of the package. If I don't get a deal, it's okay. And if I have to pay full price for something, well, that's okay too.

There's no doubt you will save money by using the strategies I teach in this book. But don't pressure yourself to invest hours and hours clipping coupons to save 90 percent off your grocery bill every time. If you save 50 percent or less, fabulous! But if couponing starts cutting into the time you could be spending with your family, working, doing something you love, or taking care of yourself, it's too much. I'm not willing to accept being secluded in a room couponing for twelve hours just for a lower grocery bill. And I'm pretty sure you aren't, either.

And another thing. If you're worried that you aren't a coupon kind of girl, don't. You don't have to be in love with coupons. You don't have to do complicated math in your head. And you don't have to set aside hours each week just to work on your coupons. I can't stress enough—balance is the key to making couponing work for you. You have to figure out how to make it fit into your world; it cannot become your world. There's no doubt that when you coupon using the strategies in this book, your life will change for the better. And there's no doubt that the savings are real, the opportunities to give are amazing, and it doesn't have to take hours a week that you don't have.

From Coupons to Workshops

I would have never imagined how God was going to take my personal experience of financial struggles and use it as a catalyst for the calling and purpose he had for me. As I continued to embrace using coupons for my family, people around me began to take notice. Shoppers behind me in the checkout line would follow me to the car and ask how they could save as much money as I was saving. I shared my strategies with them and listened to their heartbreaking stories of lost jobs, foreclosed homes, mounting medical bills, and other difficulties. I knew that what I had spent hours piecing together and learning through serious trial and error could drastically alter their finances as it had mine.

And so began the journey of Time 2 $ave. God has worked in my life and this community in such a special way. I've learned that his ways are usually not my ways, but his ways are always best. He's taught me many lessons along the way, perhaps the most important being how I can bless others in creative ways I was not able to do or even think of before I started this journey.

Save to Give, Not Just to Get

My favorite part of the workshops is the response I get when I share stories of how others have influenced and been influenced by our focus on giving. When I started accumulating a huge stockpile of stuff, there came a point when I felt guilty. I had more body wash, makeup, and other toiletries than I knew what to do with. God put it on my heart to take a box, fill it to the top with all the excess toiletries I could find, and donate it to a local battered women's shelter. He didn't stop there. Through his promptings, I was able to donate my stockpile to families in the neighborhood, victims of the tornadoes that swept through our state, and nonprofit organizations.

In chapter 10 I'll share specific ideas you can use for clipping extra coupons and buying cheap items you don't normally use.

‒ ‒ ‒ ‒ ‒

Let's get started. In the following pages I'm going to teach you easy-to-follow strategies for how you can make a difference in your finances, your lifestyle, and your community. No excuses! I'm going step-by-step so you can simplify this part of your life.

You're going to learn . . .

- How to find the coupons for what your family eats
- How to understand couponing lingo
- How to use the internet to do the work for you
- How to find sale cycles and store matchups (and what they mean)
- How to reinvent your shopping strategy and toss your lists
- How to uncover the gold mine of savings in drugstores
- How to make grocery shopping fun without any stress
- How to never have to pay full price again (or at least most of the time!)

Are you ready to start saving?

> Do not fear, for I have redeemed you;
> I have summoned you by name; you are mine.

When you pass through the waters, I will be with you;
and when you pass through the rivers, they will not sweep
over you.
When you walk through the fire, you will not be burned;
the flames will not set you ablaze.
For I am the LORD your God,
the Holy One of Israel, your Savior. (Isa. 43:1–3 NIV)

ACTION STEP

Spend time reflecting on the obstacles in life and offer those challenges up to God.

Do you feel like your life has been sidetracked by situations or circumstances beyond your control? Have you gone through a season that feels like an endless valley? I sincerely hope you haven't; but if you have, I understand. In the midst of the darkness, it's hard to imagine what it would feel like to see the light shine through again. Reflect on the things that have rocked your world. Take some time and write them down; be specific. God knows. Sometimes, however, we try to bury our fears, pain, and the truth of our life. We've got to acknowledge where we are in order to know what direction we need to move.

After you've written these things down, and if you feel comfortable, spend time in prayer. Surrender your problems to God. He is more than able to do a good work in your life. He is more than able to turn the course of your life around. You are one spoken word away from entering into God's rest.

ACTION STEP

Set some goals.

I would like you to begin by writing down your goals to keep in mind as you start on this new adventure. First, take a moment to think about what you could do by saving an extra $50 a month on your groceries. It's a very doable amount! That's just $12.50 a week, but you could use that money to make a difference.

What if you were able to save an extra $100 or $200 a month? Would you make home improvements? Take a vacation? Or maybe you would start building a savings account? Keep in mind that on top of saving money every week, once you start couponing you will also find yourself with a surplus of groceries in the house, enough to start your very own stockpile.

I understand that right now you are probably sitting in a place of need and it is difficult to think beyond that, but do you know of someone else you might be able to help with your abundance? It's likely that we all know someone who is going through a rough time. What could you offer them through couponing?

Now write down your goals. Think of them often as you make your way through this book, and keep them in mind as you walk through the store. Remember, you're not learning to coupon so you can save a buck here or there. You're doing it so you can better your life and eventually the lives of those around you.

2

The Story behind the Coupon

I've got a secret to tell, one that might surprise you a bit. Are you ready? Here it goes.

Stores. Like. Coupons.

Are you shocked? I think some of you might be. While it may seem like stores view coupons as just an added hassle, they actually benefit greatly from them in terms of drumming up extra business and bringing shoppers (and their entire grocery lists) through the door. Another thing you might not know is that stores get *paid* to send in your coupons to the manufacturer. Not only is the store reimbursed for the value of the coupon, but manufacturers also give them a few extra cents to cover processing and handling for every offer redeemed. For example, I am looking at a Schick Razor coupon right now that promises $0.08 to the store for their trouble.

Can you handle one more surprise? Manufacturers like coupons too.

It's one of their favorite ways to get us to try new products and win us over as loyal customers. And it works. My friend Torrie received a coupon once for a free Swiffer 360 Duster. She ran out, got it, took it home, and fell madly in love with it. She dusted up a happy little storm—until she ran out of refills. What do you think she did next? She went out and bought more refills, just because she loved using the product.

Now listen, this girl is a cheap-o. She's probably been dusting with her husband's same old T-shirt for the last five years. Do you think she ever would've started paying for Swiffer Duster refills if that coupon hadn't fluttered into her life? So here's what I want you to understand: contrary to popular opinion, stores are not mad at shoppers who pull out their little stack of paper slips as they walk up to the register. Through coupons manufacturers gain customers, grocery stores bring in clientele, and consumers save money. Everyone benefits.

In this chapter we'll go behind the scenes to see how a coupon works. We'll look at how manufacturers and coupon clearinghouses team up to market and provide coupons to shoppers like you and me. We'll find out what happens to your coupons once you hand them over at the register. And we'll even dive into why manufacturers offer coupons in the first place.

The Story of the Coupon

That little coupon in your hand has a story. One that started long before it landed in your Sunday paper.

Here's the thing. The coupons in your paper were born months ago. They were planned and strategized and carefully placed there as part of a complex advertising campaign. To really understand this, you have to understand the *point* of a coupon. Coupons are not printed to save you money. Not in the least. Coupons are a form of advertisement. They are an enticement, something that is designed to tip the shopping scales toward a particular item and away from the competition.

Picture this: as you are casually strolling your way down the grocery aisle, every product you walk past is vying for your attention. It's like a little competition happens right before your eyes every time you stop the cart. Now it's up to you to choose the winner. You get to choose because you are the one who picks what type of toilet paper you throw in your cart and what kind of cereal you bring home for your kids.

So how do you choose?

Well, that is the million-dollar question—literally. Stores and manufacturers alike have invested buckets of money into investigating the science behind consumer shopping habits. They have analyzed product placement, shelf positioning, end caps, and aisles. They know what time of day you are likely to shop and when you will want Coke rather than juice. (Grilling season! Super Bowl! Holiday parties!) They even have a formula for when a product will go on sale and how good of a deal they should offer.

In fact, did you know that manufacturers often pay to have their products placed on a certain part of the shelf? They absolutely do! The next time you go to the store, stroll down the cereal aisle for me. Stop right in the middle of the aisle and take a look around. The cereals shelved at your eye level are the ones most likely to appeal to adults. These are the high-cost, high-profit choices that the stores *want* you to choose and they are given premium shelf space to help achieve that goal. Now look down. Not all the way down, but down a row or two, right at the eye level of the average child. See all the sugarcoated goodness and bright colors? Those cereals are placed at that level to entice your children. Stores want children to see the box, grab the box, and want the box. It's truly a well thought-out plan, and it works.

The reality is that each week when you roam the aisles of your favorite store, you are making your way through a maze of well-laid plans and carefully crafted advertisements. The aesthetically pleasing end caps call to you as you pass them, sale tags hang from every shelf, and the coupons tucked away in your purse are whispering that you should choose their product over the one sitting next to it. It's coming at you from all sides!

Even the items you put in your cart are a form of advertisement because they made the final cut. Now as you walk through the store other shoppers will see that you chose Quaker Oatmeal, Peter Pan Peanut Butter, and Pillsbury Crescent Rolls. These are the products that came out victorious in the advertising war. And believe it or not, seeing them in your buggy does have the power to influence other shoppers, whether they realize it or not.

A Note about Sales

With all the ads swirling around on a daily basis, it might surprise you to find out that there are only three basic types of sales:

Store sales

Manufacturer sales

Manufacturer promotions

The first type of sale is the store sale. This is where the store is offering a reduced price to the consumer. Examples might include the buy one, get one (or BOGO) sales at your favorite grocery store, special pricing found in various sale flyers and weekly ads, or even store coupons. The unique thing about store sales is that they are a sort of middleman between you and the manufacturer. Stores often use these sales as a way to pass on special savings or promotions they receive from the manufacturer.

The second type of sale is a manufacturer sale. This means that the manufacturer of a product is skipping the middleman and offering special savings directly to their customers. Anyone want to guess where this type of sale shows up? You got it, coupons! Coupons are probably the best example of a manufacturer sale because the stores have absolutely nothing to do with the creation, printing, or even distribution of these little gems. We already know that coupons are a form of advertisement—all sales are—but they are one of the manufacturer's most effective tools for bringing customers into a store to buy their product. Remember, their end goal is to convince you to ignore the competition as you pluck their product from the shelf and continue on your merry way. We're okay with that; we just want them to work for it!

The last type of sale is a manufacturer promotion. Ever wonder where end caps come from? This is it! Those end caps are prime real estate, and a manufacturer will offer special pricing or kickbacks to a store if they agree to display the product in a specific location. Another example of manufacturer promotions is the special displays sprinkled throughout the store—like the blinking cardboard school bus advertising Keebler lunchbox snacks. Manufacturer promotions are a good thing because the stores often pass on these savings to the consumer in the form of a store sale. Better prices for them means better prices for us!

The Sale Cycle

The next thing to know about sales is that they cycle. Prices go up and down throughout the year, but there is a method to the madness. More often than not, every item in your favorite grocery store is on a twelve-week sale cycle. During that time the price will peak and it will plummet. The idea is to take advantage of the plummet so you can save yourself from having to splurge when the numbers start to rise.

Let me give you an example. My family loves rice. It's filling, it's easy to cook, and you can make it about a million different ways. Seriously, what's not to love? Well, there is this one kind of rice I really like that sells for about $1.00 a bag. It's one of those things that I know we are going to use, so I always seem to be throwing it into the cart week after week.

And then I started couponing. Not only that, but for the first time in my life I started paying attention to the price on the shelf and noting how it would move from week to week. One day my favorite rice would be $0.99 a bag. The next week the price would jump up to $1.29 a bag for the same exact rice. Still the next week I would see the price drop again, but this time down to $0.89 a bag. I thought the price was just fluctuating; I had no idea it was part of a sales cycle.

When I learned to wait for that rock-bottom price and then to pair it with a coupon, it was like the sky opened up and the angels started to sing. I'm telling you, I had a "Hallelujah" moment right there in the middle of the grocery store. We all know my ketchup story!

But if ketchup taught me how to coupon, rice taught me about price tracking. Because that same bag of rice fluctuates a whopping 30 percent throughout the twelve-week sale cycle. This means you can save yourself a pretty nice percentage without ever clipping the first coupon. All you have to do is be aware of the sale cycle and get to know the lowest prices on items you buy often. Oh, and my rice?

Now I usually get it for free because more often than not there is a $0.50 off coupon floating around that I can put to *very* good use.

Where Do Coupons Fit In?

Knowing about different types of sales and how the sale cycle works is important. But what does it have to do with couponing? Everything. If you want to make coupons work for you, and I mean *really* work for you, then these sales are going to play a huge role in the process. The idea being to find that rock-bottom price and *then* pull out your coupons. Pair the coupon with the sale and watch your grocery bill dwindle away.

Remember my rice? If I used my $0.50 coupon (which my store will double to $1.00) when the price is sitting at $1.29, then I still end up paying $0.29 per bag. Not a bad price. But also not the *best* price. If I use that same coupon when the price is at its lowest point of $0.89, then I snag my rice for *free*.

Let's look at another example: pasta! Let's say my favorite brand of pasta is regularly $1.68 a box. Again, not bad. But if you wait until that same box is buy one, get one free, the price drops to $0.84. Now when you use your $0.50 coupon (which your store may double to $1.00) you are walking out the door with *free* pasta.

Want to look at something a little pricier? How about diapers? This is a sale I have taken advantage of many times, and it saved me *tons* of money when I started couponing and still had little ones in diapers. In my area, Huggies diapers are around $11.99 at their peak or highest price, and during a sale they could plummet to as low as $7.99. If I waited for Huggies to be $7.99 and used a $2.00 coupon I was able to buy a pack for $5.99. That felt awesome! But in order to really make it count, I started buying enough packs of diapers during the low $7.99 price to last me until the sale cycle would bring it back to its lowest point all over again. I used coupons on every pack to pay just $5.99 each. When purchasing several packs—let's say ten—that could mean a difference of paying $59.90 versus $119.90.

We can keep doing these types of examples all day long, but the bottom line is to watch for the absolute lowest price on your favorite items and *then* buy them using your coupons. If you're worried at this point, don't be. Remember that we'll also be tracking these sales for you at Time 2 $ave.

What Happens to My Coupons after I Use Them?

Okay, you're all stocked up with a cart full of diapers and are ready to check out. You scan your items, hand over your coupons, and dance out the door thinking about all the money you just saved. But then what? After you hand your coupons over at the register you might think they simply end up gracing the bottom of a cardboard box somewhere, but their journey isn't finished yet. Once your coupons are scanned, they still have to be redeemed by the store. Next stop? The coupon clearinghouse!

Each week, someone at the store sits down to sort through all the coupons. Different coupons have to be sent to different places, and each one must be accounted for. If a coupon is sent to the wrong clearinghouse then the store won't be compensated.

The clearinghouses tally up what the different stores are owed and pass that information on to the manufacturers. The manufacturers then reimburse the stores for the value of the coupons plus about 8 cents each. Which means the store not only won your business, they also made a little money by accepting your coupon. At the end of the day, coupons are a good thing for a store's bottom line and they know it.

Now that we've gone behind the scenes to look at the life cycle of a coupon, let's just take a moment to review. A coupon starts as a promotion from the manufacturer to the consumer, one designed to get you into the store and help tip the scales in favor of their own product. It then becomes a tool you can use to lower your weekly grocery bill. You'll maximize those savings by matching the coupon with a sale going on at your store (what we call a "store matchup"). That's where the coupon becomes a source of income for the store, helping them to boost sales by bringing customers through the door. Everyone benefits. There is no downside here, so don't be nervous or ashamed to walk into the store with a handful of coupons to use.

In the next chapters we will dig deeper into the *why* and *how* of couponing. We will get down to the nitty-gritty, and you'll be a seasoned pro before we are finished. You know why coupons are printed in the first place and you now recognize that there is a best time to use them. You're already ahead of the game! Not to mention you are light years ahead of where I was when I did a public happy dance over a $0.16 bottle of ketchup.

- - - - - - - - - - - - **ACTION STEP** - - - - - - - - - - - -

Go on a scavenger hunt!

Take a little trip to your local grocery and walk around with the ad in hand. Try to identify all of the following types of promotions as you stroll the aisles:

1. *Store sale.* Look for buy one, get one free items, or items that are simply on sale this week. Pay attention to how your store prices BOGO sales. Is the price divided in half between the two items, or is one item free and the other full price?
2. *Manufacturer sale.* Try to find coupons in your store. Look for the little blinking machines, tear pads in the aisles, or coupons attached to products themselves.
3. *Manufacturer promotion.* Look for end caps or special card-board displays featuring limited-time savings.

Change Your Mind, Change Your Cart

Let's take a minute or two and go back to the beginning of our journey. Way back to the part where we all admit we have tried using coupons before and it just didn't work. No excuses, no finger-pointing; it just wasn't successful. I mean, otherwise *why* would you be reading this book?

Honey, I've heard it all. Seriously, I already know what you are going to say, and I can probably tell you what the problem is before you say a word.

Let's see if I'm close. In fact, I'll take things one step further and say here's how to fail for sure:

- You start by cutting out the weekly inserts and sticking the coupons in an envelope to keep in your purse. Even better, forget the envelope and use the inside pocket of your purse. After all, that baby is an endless black hole into which all coupons go to die.

- Next, make out your grocery list. Take a quick cruise through the fridge and the cupboards to see what you need and what you are out of. Are there any coupons that match up with your list?

Don't know . . . you'll worry about that later, probably at the store.

- Once you make it to the store, grab the items on your list and try to remember what coupons you have hiding down in your purse. Then, if you happen to think of a match, grab the coupon and stick it in a different pocket until you make your way to the checkout counter.

Waaaiiiiittt . . .

Do you see the flaw in this logic? Shopping this way means that we are expecting the coupons stuffed randomly in our purses to magically match up with the items we toss in our carts on a weekly basis. That is, when we remember to use them at all.

Insanity is defined as doing the same thing over and over yet expecting a different result. So it's time to break the cycle, try something new, and change our thinking. Time to rewire the way we shop and take advantage of all those amazing savings we always hear about but never seem to find.

In this chapter we are going to talk about the importance of changing your mindset in order to revitalize the way you shop. Then we will take things one step further as we leverage these changes into real and lasting savings. It might not be easy; these are ingrained habits that can be hard to break. If you stick with me on this, you will finally see the difference in both your grocery bill and your pantry.

Change Your Thinking

How do you typically shop for groceries? What do you do when you need toilet paper? When you need salad dressing, cereal, or dishwashing detergent? Let me guess. You write it down on a list and go to the store, right? Well, you're in the majority. Most people shop that way. But when you want to decrease your spending and increase your savings, you have to change your approach.

In the interest of full disclosure, I have to tell you that this is probably the hardest part for most people. The reason being that we have all been trained to shop a certain way. Basically we go to the store every week with a list based on what we *need* right then. A list made up of the items we feel we will use in a given week that are not currently in our cabinets or pantries. The problem with this approach is that it doesn't allow us to capitalize on sales, special pricing, coupons, or any other type of deal. It is a need-based approach, pure and simple.

Now, what I challenge you to do is to stop shopping based on what you *need* and start shopping based on what you *use*. Believe it or not, there is a pretty big difference between the two!

When you shop based on use, you are taking advantage of the various types of sales to find that rock-bottom price on the items you know and love. Instead of starting in your pantry and making a list of all the empty holes, you start with the sale ads and work your way back to the pantry.

At this point I want to walk you through a few examples to fully explain what I'm talking about. Keep in mind that while we will dive into the basics of "Couponing 101" in the next chapter, for now we are focusing on why the strategy works. We will get into how it works very soon, but first I have to explain the method behind the madness.

For example, let's say that Publix currently has Yoplait YoPlus Yogurt on sale BOGO. These particular yogurts are normally $2.00 each and your kids love them. In fact, they love them so much that you find yourself tossing a pack or two into the cart each week whether they are on sale or not. Today, when you see that they are only $1.00, you might buy an extra pack as a special treat.

Does this sound familiar? Yep, that was me just a few short years ago!

The above scenario describes need-based shopping. You buy two or three packs because you will need two or three packs this week. And what about the future? Well, you'll need more next week, so you'll probably find yourself walking down this same aisle again whether yogurt is on sale or not.

Now let's look at this same scenario from a use-based approach.

As you are looking through the sale ads you find that Yoplait YoPlus Yogurt is on sale BOGO for $1.00 each. You know that your family *uses* this yogurt, so you flip through your coupons to find that there is a $0.50 off one Yoplait YoPlus, which Publix will double to $1.00 off one. Meaning that you can combine the store sale (the BOGO) with the manufacturer's sale (the coupon) to bring home *free* yogurt for your family this week. And if you happen to have five of the same coupon, then you can bring home five free packs of yogurt. This takes care of what your family will *need* this week and what they will *use* next week. It also takes yogurt off your shopping list for the next few weeks and frees up part of your budget for something else.

For another example let's look at Peter Pan Peanut Butter.

If you were to *need* peanut butter this week, then it would cost you roughly $3.69 for a small jar.

But did you know that last week Peter Pan Peanut Butter was BOGO? That same peanut butter that you will pay almost $4.00 for today you could have purchased for less than $2.00 just seven days ago. You didn't *need* it then, but you do *use* it and you could have used that sale to save you money.

Here is how the math breaks down:

Need-Based Example: Peter Pan Peanut Butter

Need peanut butter	$3.69 regular price
Coupon? Yes!	$0.50 off 1
Final price:	$2.69 if the store doubles
	$3.19 if the store doesn't double

Use-Based Example: Peter Pan Peanut Butter

Need peanut butter	$3.69 (BOGO) = $1.85 each
Coupon? Yes!	$0.50 off 1
Final price:	$0.85 if the store doubles
	$1.35 if the store doesn't double

So pay $2.69 out of pocket (OOP) today when you *need* the peanut butter, *or* pay $0.85 a week earlier when you only knew that you would *use* it. Which would you choose? The lesson here is simple. Why pay more for something later that you can pay much less for today?

Let's go one step further. To fully take advantage of these types of savings, we need to purchase enough to last our family about twelve weeks, or until the item goes on sale again. (Remember the whole twelve-week sale cycle? This is where that comes into play.) How much you purchase depends on how much your family uses. Plus, I encourage you to look beyond your family and pick up extra where you can just for the purpose of giving.

It's time to look at our peanut butter example one more time, but now we are shopping to stock up for twelve full weeks. Let's say that your family uses one jar of peanut butter per week.

Stock-up Example: Twelve-week Supply of Peanut Butter

Peanut butter on sale	$1.85
Jar per week x 12 weeks	$22.20
Price after coupon savings ($0.85 each if store doubles) ($1.35 each if store does not double)	$10.20 $16.20
Regular price for same product ($3.69 each)	$44.28

See the difference? By shopping ahead based on what your family will use you saved $34.08 on one single item. That is $12.00 of savings from using manufacturer's coupons if your store doubles coupons, or $6.00 if it does not double coupons, and an additional $22.08 from taking advantage of the store's BOGO sale. I point this out to say that it isn't one type of sale or the other that really makes the big difference. The secret to saving the most is using the two together.

So what if you changed the way you shopped? Imagine multiplying these types of savings throughout your entire weekly grocery list. Instead of need, usage should determine what goes on your list. If you start thinking differently about what you use, you will see results instantly.

Still not convinced? Let's look at a few more examples.

Item	Regular Price	BOGO Sale Price	Coupon	Final Price w/ Doubling*	Final Price w/o Doubling
Crystal Light	$3.30	$1.65	$0.50 off 1	$0.65	$1.15
Rice-A- Roni (2)	$1.50	$0.75	$1.00 off 2	(2) $0.50	(2) $0.50
Pasta	$1.60	$0.80	$0.50 off 1	FREE	$0.30
Frozen veggies	$2.85	$1.43	$0.50 off 1	$0.43	$0.93
Cereal	$4.22	$2.11	$0.50 off 1	$1.11	$1.61
Total OOP	$13.47	$6.74		$2.69	$4.49

*Store doubles coupons up to $0.50.

The examples in the table above represent recent sales in my area. I didn't just pull them out of thin air and slap them down on paper.

They are real numbers and real savings that anyone can take advantage of. Just look at the totals; do you see the huge differences between the amount of money it would cost to bring home the exact same groceries? The only difference? Shopping smart and being willing to shop based on what you will use rather than what you need.

Here is the cost breakdown for these items purchased four different ways:

Regular price total	$13.47
BOGO sale total	$6.74
Sale total + coupons	$4.49
Sale total + double coupons	$2.69

In this example, shopping based on use at a store that doubles coupons would save you over 80 percent. That's huge! And I realize that not everyone lives near a store that doubles coupons. Don't let that discourage you! In the same example you would still save over 65 percent off your total bill without doubling the first coupon. Still a substantial savings and still a number to get excited about.

Now, what if you bought enough of each item to last you until the next sale cycle? (Remember, twelve weeks—or about three months from now.) Do you realize what that would do to your grocery bill? Moreover, do you realize what that would do to your weekly shopping list? I sure hope so! It would change . . . drastically! At this point you don't and won't *need* pasta, rice, frozen veggies, cereal, Rice-A-Roni, or Crystal Light for at least the next three months. These items are off your list and you now have the luxury of waiting for another fantastic price before you buy them again.

Remember when I told you my ketchup story? I had no idea what I was doing back then. I was just excited to get a good deal. I didn't even realize that I was buying enough ketchup, salsa, or whatever else to last until it went on sale again. Didn't even cross my mind. However, what I did notice was that after a while my list began to shrink. Suddenly, items like ketchup, salsa, spaghetti sauce, salad dressing, laundry detergent, dishwasher tablets, frozen veggies, snacks, and pasta were off my list. Why? Because without realizing it I was building a nice stockpile and wouldn't need these items again for several weeks. My shopping habits were changing all on their own before it finally dawned on me what had happened. I was taking advantage of the low price and buying enough of the items my family used, and then I could wait until it went on sale again.

I know this is going to be hard for some of you. I warned you about that right from the beginning. The truth is that we are comfortable with the way we shop. It's probably how our mothers shopped and it's what we know. But it's not the way to save money. Shopping based on use is different; I understand that. I also understand that you have to try something different if you want to see a different result. The only question is, are you willing to try? I sure hope so.

In the next section we are going to talk about price tracking and how you can use this strategy to lower your weekly bill without ever using the first coupon. It takes some time to get the hang of it, but this goes hand in hand with a use-based shopping approach, one that will save you both time and money in the long run. I realize you don't know how this is all going to shake out yet, and that's okay. We are taking things in little bites. We can't tackle an entire lifetime of shopping habits overnight. It's a process, but it's worth it.

Price Tracking

You know that you are looking for the lowest price. That part is pretty straightforward. The tricky part is knowing what that price is and how to find it. It's not a sprint, or even a marathon. It's a system that can, and probably will, change the way you shop. Even if you never use the first coupon, understanding this important concept has the potential to dramatically reduce your grocery bill.

First off, I want you to grab a copy of your grocery list. Take a few minutes and jot down beside each item what you think is the approximate price. Don't worry if you don't know; I had no idea how much items cost nor did I think it was necessary for me to know. If, for example, I needed milk or toilet paper, then the price didn't matter. What mattered was that I needed it and my family wasn't going to be very happy with me if I came home without it. It's not like I can hold out and not buy toilet paper for a week or two while I wait for it to go on sale!

My savings strategy was simple. Are you ready for this? If I needed something, I simply walked up, scanned the shelf for the cheapest item that still looked decent, and dropped it in the cart. My philosophy being that I have to buy it anyway, and if I need it I need it. I didn't even know there was another option. In my mind the price was comparable at most grocery stores and I was doing my best. That brings to mind the Scripture verse that says, "My people are destroyed from lack of knowledge" (Hos. 4:6 NIV). I had a lack of knowledge and I didn't even realize it. Just think of how many families right now are not merely surviving but thriving simply because they learned to use coupons effectively.

Ever wonder what thriving looks like?

- It's the changing mindset of the first-time mother who is working full-time while trying to balance life and save money.
- It's the changing attitude of the single mother of two who without any child support is able to move from running on empty and feeling hopeless to being full and feeling filled with joy.
- It's the changing giving habits of the older couple who used to donate only on special holidays and now find a purpose in giving to their community each week.
- It's the changing circumstance of a one-income family of five whose father lost his job, whose home was foreclosed, and who went from relying on food stamps to having more than enough for a whole lot less.

These stories represent just a few of the many men and women who attend Time 2 $ave couponing workshops. People of all ages, backgrounds, and financial and family situations have something to share about how couponing made a difference in their lives. And it's almost always about more than just building a massive stockpile. It's about change.

I have a story I'd like to share from a girl who attended one of my workshops and later was kind enough to open her heart to me.

Before I learned how to coupon there were weeks when I couldn't afford to go to the grocery store. Our reality was that my husband was laid off in November, and three months later I lost my job as well . . . all with a small child at home to think about. For the next year it was a struggle just to keep the heat on, much less anything more than the most basic of necessities. Every week I went to the store with a strict budget. I didn't have a choice; I just did the best I could. And I can't tell you how heartbreaking it is to look into your child's eyes yet again as you tell them you don't have milk. You don't have bread or peanut butter or whatever common, inexpensive item they are asking for, and you don't know when you will be able to buy more. They forgive you, but it's much harder to forgive yourself.

Couponing changed everything. Now my cabinets are full and my weekly grocery bill is a fraction of what it once was. Plus, I sleep peacefully at night not having to worry about putting food on the table, and it feels great to be able to pull a bag of Goldfish crackers out and hand them over to that sweet, smiling face anytime she asks. Our finances are better now, but this is a skill I will always use and always be grateful for.

I love hearing stories like this. It's amazing to see how something that can seem so trivial has the power to make such a difference in the lives of others. You probably haven't realized this yet, but here's a secret for you: coupons = cash. Basically you have two choices: you can spend your cash or use coupons. The choice is yours.

Which brings us back to price tracking. Before I had my ketchup moment, I never succeeded in saving my family any real money. My intentions were good, but it seemed that no matter what I bought, my bill was always the same. First it was always $100 a week. Then the number started to rise, slowly but steadily, until it tipped over the $150 mark and I knew I had to do something to stop the madness. That "something" was couponing, and I have never looked back.

Back then, while I noticed that prices would vary slightly from week to week, it just wasn't something that I paid attention to. It was more of an, *Oh look! Cheerios are $3.50 this week. Hmm . . . weren't they cheaper last week?* And then the thought would be gone and I would happily move on to the next item. Why? Because it was a random thing to me. I had no idea there was a twelve-week sale cycle or that I should even be paying attention to things like that.

What? You too? I totally get it. After all, when we are going through grade school and then high school and even college, no one ever pulls you aside and says, "Hey, let me teach you how to shop." It just doesn't happen, and that's where this book comes into play. We've already covered the twelve-week cycle, so let's just say that if an item is on sale this week, it is safe to assume the price will be higher next week.

Once upon a time I attempted not only to price track every single item on my list but also keep track of the prices at every single store in my area. Crazy! What I quickly figured out was that I don't have to make this process harder than it is. I don't have to build a huge spreadsheet that tracks more variables than an air traffic controller. I don't have to know the exact price of every item at every store. I don't have to figure it all out on my own.

So what's the secret to this entire price tracking thing? Well, there are two options.

First, you can go to our blog at Time2SaveWorkshops.com. We get rid of the guesswork by only posting the best deals each week. You don't have to know in advance what to look for, but you will start to notice patterns. Certain items will be cheaper at certain times of the year while others tend to pop up more frequently. The site is constantly updated and we do everything possible to always post the best and most reliable information we have. In short, we know you've got a lot to handle and we want to make things just a little bit easier for you.

Second, if you don't want to use the website you can just make a list of your core items and keep track from week to week. But keep it simple and manageable. By keeping track of only the most important items, you lower your workload and keep yourself from burning out.

Now, let go of worrying about price tracking. I know some of you are feeling anxious right now because either you have no idea what anything costs or you're a spreadsheet person and need a concrete formula that you can see. Keep holding on; the journey will be worth it.

Think back to the last time you checked out at the grocery store. How did you feel when the cashier announced your total? Were you excited or happy? Did you feel a sense of accomplishment of a job well done? Did you feel challenged? Or did you feel frustrated, annoyed, stressed, and overwhelmed? Here's your chance. You have two doors standing in front of you: door A and door B. It's up to you which one you take. Door A is familiar; you already know the outcome. Door B is a little scary because you've never been there before and it will force you to change. That can be uncomfortable at even the best of times, but if you stick with it, you'll see results.

The first thing to keep in mind is the end goal: to save your family money and open doors to giving. The goal is *not* to have the best savings average, the biggest stockpile, or the most coupons. Going to the grocery store is a necessary part of our lives; however, it doesn't have to control us. It's not necessary to trade sanity for free groceries. Honey, between you and me, we've got enough things threatening our sanity on a daily basis! Keep in mind (and if you don't, I will continue to remind you!), whether you save 5 percent, 10 percent, or 50 percent, it's still money that you saved. It's still money that your family gets to keep in your pocket. No matter how much or how little you save, you are successful.

ACTION STEP

Do your research.

Pull out the weekly ad for a store you usually shop at, or find their weekly ad online. Look for just one item your family uses on a regular basis that seems to be at least half off the price you normally pay. Now burn it into your memory, because this is going to be your first adventure in use-based shopping. This week, without even touching the first coupon, buy an extra two or three of this item during your shopping trip. Next week when the price jumps back up to normal, you can smile as you pass right on by, knowing you have plenty at home and now have the luxury of holding out for a better deal.

4

Couponing 101

Understanding the *HOW*

All right, before we jump headfirst into a shopping trip, we've got to cover the basics. Are you ready for this? After all, there is much more to a coupon than just snagging X amount off of an item or two. Knowing how to read a coupon, as well as knowing how to put it to good use, is a big deal because it can save you quite a bit in terms of both money and headaches.

In this chapter we are going to look at the *how* of couponing. As in, how do you differentiate between types of coupons? How do you know what the different parts of a coupon mean? How do you stack coupons together to get the best deal? How do you understand all the couponing lingo that everyone is slinging out? And how do you use these little treasures in the first place?

It's a lot to cover, I know that! Remember, I'm the girl who was completely stoked about a super cheap bottle of ketchup. But I also know that you can do it. And once we are done with these next few pages, you will be well ahead of where I was when I first got started. You'll know the basics. You'll have the tools. All that will be left is putting them to good use.

What Is a Coupon?

What is a coupon? Is it a little slip of paper printed to save you money? No, but we know that already. We know that a coupon represents a sale directly from the manufacturer to the consumer. What we haven't covered is how to capitalize on that sale so you can get the best possible price for your family. The first step is understanding the parts of a coupon. The second step is being able to tell the difference between store and manufacturer coupons. Seems pretty straightforward, doesn't it? In this section we will explore the parts and types of coupons as we learn how to maximize our savings and use them to the fullest.

Parts of a Coupon

Coupons have a lot to say. They're tiny but loud! I mean, seriously, those manufacturers manage to pack quite the punch onto a few scant inches of print. We're talking expiration dates, discount amounts, purchase requirements, redemption addresses, and bar codes. And that's before we even touch on the pictures. Who knew a coupon had so much to say?

I know this may seem like a small piece of the puzzle, but if you don't understand each part of a coupon and the role it plays, then you are dooming yourself to fail before you ever really get started. Yep, it's often the little things that matter. So let's take a minute to dig in and dissect a coupon.

Item

The first thing to look at is the item listed on the coupon. And this means both the picture and the title. Why does this matter? Because these two facets tell you what the coupon is for. They outline what product or products this particular coupon can be redeemed on and they help you to quickly identify what you have. One thing to keep in mind: the title matters more than the picture. I tell you this because sometimes the picture and the wording will not match exactly.

For example, let's say that the picture shows one large 64-ounce bottle of Strawberry Banana V8 Splash juice drink. At first glance you might think that this picture fully represents the coupon. But when you read the wording you notice that this particular coupon is for "$1.00 off *any* V8 Splash juice drink."

Big difference. And one that you might miss if you don't take a moment to read what the coupon has to say. So you know how they always tell you to read the fine print? This is one time when that habit will definitely work to your advantage.

Value

What is it worth? That's what we all want to know, right? The value of a coupon lets us know how much that particular coupon saves us. It's pretty straightforward and will look something like this:

- $0.30 off 1 Pillsbury Crescent Rolls
- $0.40 off 2 Pillsbury Crescent Rolls
- $0.40 off 2 Pillsbury Crescent or Sweet Rolls

If you look at these examples you will notice that they vary slightly. Remember, the wording matters. In a sense, the wording outlines just how good the value will be. In the first example you would receive $0.30 off any one Pillsbury Crescent Roll. Meaning that this coupon could be redeemed for any Pillsbury Crescent Roll you could find. Easy, right?

The second coupon could only be used if you bought two Pillsbury Crescent Rolls. Where before you just needed to pay attention to a general brand category, now quantity comes into play.

Value matters for a couple reasons. First off, not all coupons are created equal, and this depends greatly on the stores in your area and their own unique coupon policy. If you shop at a store that doubles coupons up to a certain amount, then some coupons will end up being much more valuable than they first appear. For example, in my area Publix doubles all manufacturer coupons up to $0.50. This means that a $0.40 coupon that doubles to $0.80 will end up being more valuable than a $0.55 coupon that will not double at all.

How do you know if your store doubles? You ask. Coupon policies have a tendency to change without warning, and the only way you can stay on top of the latest and greatest deals is to check with customer service or research their policy on the store website. Plus, it's always good to have a printed version of the policy with you when you shop. This helps a ton if you ever have any issues or questions at the register.

Barcode

The barcode is the bit of the coupon that makes the whole thing work. In most cases, if the barcode won't scan, then the coupon gets the boot. Now, I will admit that there are a few exceptions to this rule with store coupons, but it is always a good rule of thumb to take care of your barcodes and keep them whole.

I won't get into a long spiel about what a barcode looks like; we've all seen our share. What you need to pay attention to is how many barcodes are on a coupon. We will cover this more in-depth once we start talking about different types of coupons, but just know that manufacturer coupons always have at least one barcode, while store coupons might not have a barcode at all.

Expiration Date

The expiration date is crucial. Why? Because they simply won't work if you try to use them after that magical date has passed.

Confession time: this isn't something I used to pay much attention to. My thought was that the register would catch it if I didn't and let me know. It wasn't until much later that I learned how many coupons would still scan far beyond their expiration date.

The reality is that stores can't redeem expired coupons. They may scan at the register, but the store ends up taking a hit and it's money lost for them. So let's do the right thing here. We don't need to rely on the register or the cashier to be our moral compass. That's something we should take care of all on our own. These types of savings come with an expiration date, one that is clearly marked and that we all need to pay attention to.

Did you know that expired coupons aren't trash?
It's true!

Military families overseas are allowed to use coupons up to 6 months past their printed expiration date! After your coupons have expired gather them together to send overseas. This is a great activity to involve your kids in as it opens up the opportunity to have a conversation about the sacrifices our military makes for our freedom.

Redemption Address

Right smack in the middle of most coupons you will find a fairly large section of teeny, tiny print that no one cares to read. And you don't have to. You just have to make sure that the store can read it because this section outlines where they have to send the coupon as well as how much they will receive for it. If a coupon has a redemption address, it's always a manufacturer coupon.

In the next chapter we are going to ice this cake as we look at different ways to organize our coupons. Trust me, there's a system out there for everyone. Even my ants-in-the-pants, ADHD, can't-sit-still-to-save-my-life self! For now, let's just say that depending on which organization method you choose, stapling might be part of the system and you'll need to be careful not to staple the redemption address. Why? Because your coupons can tear a bit at the spot where they're stapled. If this happens to be the redemption address, then the store will not be able to read it and they may not accept the coupon. So just be mindful and know that the tiny print has big importance.

Types of Coupons

In the world of coupons there are two types: store and manufacturer. The difference is who distributes the coupon. Store coupons are printed by individual stores and, barring specific coupon policies, can only be used at that store or chain of stores. Manufacturer coupons are distributed by manufacturers and can be used anywhere that accepts coupons and sells that specific product.

How can you tell the difference between the two? First, most store coupons will be labeled with the store name and will state that the coupon can be redeemed only at BI-LO or Publix or Walgreens, for example. You get the picture. But the real test is the redemption address. If a coupon has a redemption address, it's always a manufacturer coupon. This is the most simple way to differentiate between a manufacturer and a store coupon. Unlike manufacturer coupons, stores are not reimbursed for the value of a store coupon. Instead it comes out of their marketing budget.

So it's really a simple test. No redemption address? Store coupon. Redemption address? Manufacturer coupon. Even if it says otherwise.

This is important because (1) you need to know if specific coupons will be accepted at your favorite store; and (2) many stores will permit you to stack store and manufacturer coupons, allowing you to score an even better price on certain items.

A quick note on store coupons and store policy. When you shop, make sure to ask about your store's policy on store coupons. The reason I point this out is because some stores will allow you to use a single store coupon *multiple* times. You can hand them one coupon and tell them that you would like to use it three times. It is a policy that varies from store to store, but it is very handy when it pops up.

Where Do Coupons Live?

Now that you know what to look for, it's time to talk about where to find them. See, coupons often hide in plain sight and couponers have created a lingo all their own. One that can make it a bit difficult for the average newbie to figure out what they are talking about! I mean, it's not uncommon to hear people rattling off about IPs, peelies, blinkies, BOGO, WAGS, SS, RP, and even PG.

Makes total sense, right?

Let me break it down for you:

IP—Internet printable

Peelie—Peelable coupon found on an individual product

Blinkie—Flashing (or *blinking*) box attached to grocery store shelves that dispenses coupons

BOGO—Buy one, get one sale

WAGS—Walgreens

MFR or MQ—Manufacturer coupon

SS—Smart Source

RP—Red Plum

PG—Proctor & Gamble

And this is just the start. In the next chapter we are going to break this down big-time by looking in-depth at each type of coupon and where to find it. (By the way, if you flip to the back of this book you will find a handy dandy appendix stocked with a ready-made couponing glossary.) Before we're through, we'll have you speaking coupon lingo like a pro.

Couponing Basics

At this point you know how to read a coupon like the back of your hand. You know what it's for, when it expires, and even where you can use it. So now we need to talk about *how* to use it. This is the part that can trip people up, and the main reason it can feel so confusing is that every store is different. Literally, each store will have its own coupon policy.

Clear as mud, right? Actually, it's not that bad. It's just a matter of asking the right questions before you start. And the best place to find answers and guidance is at the customer service counter of your favorite store. Want to know the store's coupon policy? Ask. Need help understanding that policy? Ask. Want someone to clarify the language in the sale ad? *Ask!* It won't bother them. Stores love couponers who make the effort to understand the policy and abide by it. It makes them happy. So be that couponer, step out of your comfort zone, and ask for help if you need it. It will definitely be worth it.

Just ask my friend Amy. Amy loves to talk about one of her first coupon trips. She knew that she had all the right coupons, she just wasn't sure how to use them. What did she end up doing? Well, the store wasn't crowded that day, so she spread out all her coupons right there at the checkout stand and asked for help. And if you knew Amy, you would know that she is just so sweet and so innocent that you can't help but love her on sight. The cashiers laughed as they explained about the different types of coupons and how she could use them to get the best deal. Amy walked out that day with a great price on her groceries *and* two new friends at the store. She now looks for these ladies every time she shops and to this day they are still happy to see her.

That is what I hope for you: that this process will enrich your life, not make it harder. It can!

Shorthand

As you read through the rest of this chapter, and throughout the rest of the book, you will notice a type of couponing shorthand being used. The same shorthand is sprinkled throughout the Time 2 $ave blog and just about any place you find people talking about coupons. Remember when I said that couponers have their own language? This is just one more example. Only now we have mastered a written as well as a spoken form!

But what does it all mean? Simple! I'll be happy to break it down for you as we decode the lingo once and for all. Here is our first example.

Let's say your local grocery store has Vitamin Water on sale 10 for $10. If this were the case, then you might see a note on the blog that looked something like this:

Vitamin Water 10/$10
Use $0.50/1 Vitamin Water, tear pad
(makes it $0.50 each or FREE if store doubles)

Now let's break it down. The first part is easy, Vitamin Water is on sale 10 for $10, or $1.00 each. (Quick note: with 10 for $10 sales, most of the time you don't have to buy a set amount to get the price. Just look at the items as if they are on sale for $1.00 each.) Next, we have the coupon. When you see a price followed by a forward slash and a number, this is shorthand for the value of the coupon. This particular coupon is worth $0.50 off one Vitamin Water. The last section of the line tells you where you can find the coupon. In this case it was a tear pad. The notes in parentheses let you know the final price after coupons.

Here's another example:

Jolly Time Popcorn BOGO $1.99 ($1.00)
Use $0.50/1 Jolly Time Popcorn, RP 01/12
(makes it $0.50 each or FREE if store doubles)

In this case we are talking about a BOGO sale for Jolly Time Popcorn. The popcorn is regularly $1.99, but because it's buy one, get one free, it's $1.00 each when you buy two (wyb 2). The second line tells us that you can find a coupon for $0.50 off one Jolly Time Popcorn in the Red Plum insert from January 12.

The good news is that this type of shorthand is pretty standard. Once you have the hang of it, you can cruise your way through the internet and make yourself right at home no matter what couponing site you happen to come across. (And if you get lost, just pull out this book. Appendix C is stocked with all the shortcuts you could ever need.)

BOGO

One of the most common types of sales in grocery stores is buy one, get one free, or BOGO. Now, I'm pretty sure you know what this is. But what you might not know is that many times grocery store BOGO's are quite different from the more traditional type of BOGO that we are used to.

A traditional BOGO requires that you buy one item for full price and receive the second item for free. So you could buy a pair of shoes for $19.99 and then pay zilch for the second pair. In this type of sale, because the second item is already free, you could only use one coupon. It would look something like this:

First box of cereal	$4.00
Second box of cereal	FREE
Use (1) $0.50/1 MFR	-$0.50
Final price	$3.50 ($1.75 each wyb 2)

However, many grocery store BOGOs are more like a 50 percent off sale. In this type of sale no item is actually *free*; instead, everything would ring up as half price. Now you can use coupons on each individual item you buy. A grocery store BOGO would then look something like this:

First box of cereal	$2.00 (BOGO price)
Second box of cereal	$2.00 (BOGO price)
Use (2) $0.50/1 MFR	-$1.00
Final price for both	$3.00 ($1.50 each wyb 2)

This type of BOGO allows you to double your coupon savings. If you're not sure what type of BOGO your store uses, just ask. It's always good to know the rules.

Doubling

After you have the store coupon policy in hand, you need to know how to make it work for you. The first thing to check is whether or not your store doubles or triples manufacturer coupons.

Doubling refers to a practice where the store will "match" the value of your coupon up to a set amount. So a $0.50 coupon would be worth $1.00 if your store doubled coupons up to $0.50. A $0.75 coupon would still be worth $0.75 in this case if they only double up to $0.50.

Most Publix stores, for example, will double all manufacturer coupons up to $0.50 while BI-LO will double up to $0.60. Other stores won't double at all, and others only double on certain days of the week or only during special "double events" or "super doubles." I know this sounds like a lot, but here's the deal: you *do not* have to know about every store. You don't. It doesn't matter what a store's policy is unless you want to shop there. Those are the only stores you need to worry about. So what would that be? Two, possibly three stores? That, my friend, is a manageable number!

If your store doubles this can increase your potential savings and it is definitely something to take advantage of. If it doesn't, don't be discouraged. After all, as we showed in the last chapter, you can still save a huge amount on your weekly bill without ever doubling a coupon.

Stacking

The next thing to check is whether or not your store will allow you to "stack" coupons. Stacking refers to the practice of using both a store and a manufacturer coupon on the same item, thus doubling your savings and stepping up your coupon game.

Okay, so we know that there are two different types of coupons floating around out there—store and manufacturer. A manufacturer coupon is created and distributed by product manufacturers to increase sales of a particular product. Consumers can use these coupons in pretty much any store. When you use this type of coupon the store will send it back to the manufacturer and get reimbursed for the value of the coupon plus a few extra cents. A store coupon is created by a specific grocery or drugstore as part of an in-house marketing campaign. When you use this type of coupon the store does not get reimbursed for it, but instead accounts for it in their marketing budget. Also, some chain stores submit their store coupons back to their corporate office for credit.

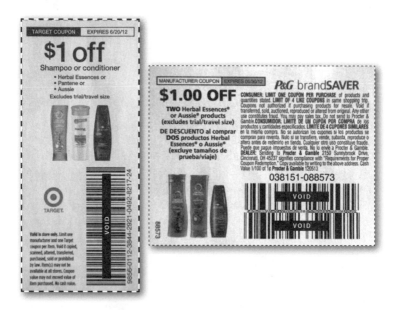

Here is where things start to get good! If you have a store and a manufacturer coupon for the same item, many stores will allow you to use both. This is called stacking. For example, if Target distributes a store coupon for shampoo, the first thing I would do is check my binder or coupon file (more on this in the next chapter). It might just be that I also have a manufacturer coupon for that very same shampoo. Combine the two and you get a double whammy.

Example 1 of Stacking

Herbal Essences on sale	$2.50 per bottle
Buy 2 bottles	$5.00
Use (1) $1.00/1 store coupon	- $1.00
Use (1) $1.00/2 MFR	- $1.00/2
Price after all coupons	$3.00 for both ($1.50 each wyb 2)

Note: In this example we needed to buy *two bottles* of shampoo to get the best deal. Why? Because our manufacturer coupon was for $1.00 off two. Buying two bottles allowed us to stack both coupons and get a better price.

Let's look at another example:

Example 2 of Stacking

All® Laundry Detergent on sale	$5.00 each for Small and Mighty
Buy 1 bottle	$5.00
Use (1) $2.00/1 MFR	-$2.00
Use (1) $1.00/1 store coupon	-$1.00
Price after all coupons	$2.00

In this example we only had to buy one bottle of laundry detergent to get the best price. The deal could be done multiple times if you had enough coupons, but both the store and the MFR were off single items.

Competitor Coupons

Yeah! The basics are done and now it's time for us to kick things up a notch or two. This time I'm talking about competitor coupons.

Competitor coupons are store coupons from a competing store. Many stores will allow you to use store coupons from other nearby, competing stores (competitor coupons), but there are limits. For example, some BI-LO stores will accept competitor coupons but only from specific stores. Also, most Publix stores will accept competitor coupons but you have to pay close attention to their policy. They only accept one "like" competitor coupon per transaction and only from stores they consider to be their competitors. Whom do they consider to be such a competitor? That varies by store and will depend on what other stores you have in your area.

I tell you this not to confuse you but to point out one more time how important it is to be familiar with store policy. It really is true that every store or chain is different, and it's up to you to know the guidelines. Many stores have a printable copy available on their website. When possible, print a copy to have on hand and get acquainted with the customer service counter. Stores love couponers who make an effort to be courteous and follow the rules.

The reason competitor coupons are so exciting is that they are still considered a store coupon, which means you can still stack them. So while BI-LO may not have a store coupon on an item they have on sale, Target might. If your BI-LO accepts competitor coupons, you can use that to your advantage and grab a really great deal.

Example of Using Competitor Coupons

Quaker Oatmeal on sale at BI-LO BOGO	$3.98 ($1.99 after BOGO)
Buy 2 boxes	$3.98 total price for both
Use (2) $0.50/1 MFR (doubled)	-$2.00
Use (1) $1.00/2 competitor coupon	-$1.00
Price after all coupons	$0.98 for both, or $0.49 each wyb 2

And that's it! You have made it through Couponing 101 and are ready to move on to the next level: organization. Don't be discouraged if you have to read through this chapter more than once. Couponing can be tricky when you first get started, and no one knows that better than me. But don't be afraid to try. Start small if you want to—one coupon, one item. Just start somewhere. Each shopping trip will leave you more self-assured, and that's the goal. You'll soon be able to walk confidently into a store and learn something new with each experience. If you can do that then you're already far ahead of the curve.

ACTION STEP

Know your store's coupon policy.

Take a second and think about your favorite place to shop. Do you know their coupon policy? If not, then this is a great time to find out. You can check the store website, give them a call, or even stop by the customer service counter. Whichever way, this is great information to have on hand *before* you ever build your first list.

5

A-Hunting We Will Go

The first thing you need to have to coupon is coupons. Makes sense, right? But where to find them? I mean, we've gone our whole shopping lives without coupons jumping out at us, so how is that supposed to change today? I know, I know! I feel your pain here. The good news is that coupons are literally everywhere.

Don't believe me? Well check this out. The latest numbers show that of the roughly $470 billion in coupons printed in 2011, only $4.6 billion were ever redeemed.[1] That's a usage rate of about 0.98 percent. What does that mean for you? It means that there are still plenty of coupons floating around just ready and waiting for you to snatch them up and put them to good use.

But where do you find them?

I can help you with that! Like so many of you, when I started out I just wasn't looking in the right places. It's all about knowing where to look. I'll show you the best spots to find the most coupons. Some places you may have already known about, but others you've probably never thought of.

---

1. Charlie Brown, "NCH Annual Topline Coupon Facts," *NCH Marketing Resource Center*, January 2012, https://www.nchmarketing.com/resourcecenter/couponknowledgestream4a.aspx?id=7317.

Where Are They Hiding?

The biggest thing to keep in mind is that coupons really are *every-where*. So much so that we have practically trained ourselves to over-look them. We are so used to seeing different types of offers that we just pass right on by without thinking twice. Special display? Steer the cart right around it. Peelie on the packaging? Toss it out with the trash.

It's time to break this cycle and snatch up these savings. Think of it as a game. Start hunting for coupons and you'll be amazed at all the places they like to pop up.

Newspapers

It may seem cliché, but newspapers are and always have been *the* place to find coupons. In fact, this is the venue where 89.6 percent of all coupons are issued.[2] So the best place to start couponing is your own hometown newspaper.

How many should you buy? Well, that's up to you. I wouldn't recommend going out and buying twenty papers, but you will prob-ably find that you do want more than one. So experiment a bit and find the number that works best for your family. That perfect amount where you can get what you need for the next twelve weeks—not the next twelve years!

I personally can't remember the first time I bought more than one newspaper. I'm sure I started off with one or two extra, a nice manageable number and definitely not enough to make the cashier look at me like I had lost my mind. I mean, one or two extra and you might just be picking one up for your mom or a neighbor. But ten? That's crazy town! (Remember, this is when I first started couponing. I no longer get ten papers as I've found that five is perfect for my family.)

However, I soon realized that if I wanted more than one bottle of ketchup, salsa, or body wash then I was going to need more than one paper. After all, more papers do mean more coupons! I remember one week in particular when the cashier asked me if I knew that all

2. Ibid.

the newspapers had the same stories. She meant well, she really did, and I still chuckle thinking about the oh-so-sincere look on her face.

One thing to keep in mind here: not every paper gets every coupon. Manufacturers advertise by zip code based on shopping habits and sales projections. So the coupons in your local paper will vary from the town down the road and many times from what we have listed at Time 2 $ave.

The best way to make sure you're getting the most newspaper coupons possible is to buy the largest paper you can. The larger the city, the more (and better) coupons you'll find inside.

Magazines

Magazines are a great place to find coupons. And not just any coupons, but often higher value coupons than what you typically find in the Sunday paper.

For instance, *All You* magazine is loaded with coupons, typically boasting $70 to $120 of savings in every issue. Each issue is packed with both time- and money-saving tips, along with fashion advice for real women, parenting pointers, recipes, and more. Other good magazines for coupons include *Better Homes & Gardens*, *Ladies Home Journal*, *Woman's Day*, and similar publications.

Stores

Stores are a breeding ground for coupons. They pop up all over the place. From peelies to special displays to Catalinas and even blinkies, you never know what you are going to find when you turn the corner and start waltzing down a new aisle. So be ready and keep your eyes peeled. After all, couponing can be lots of fun!

Another great place to find coupons at the store is the customer service counter. This is always my *first* stop as soon as I walk through the door. The store usually has a nice little stack of coupons hanging out behind the counter and all you have to do is ask. It is also the hands down best place to find store coupons and learn about special sales happening within the store itself.

In drugstores, it usually pays to stop by the cosmetics counter to ask for coupons. They often have an array of coupons for cosmetics, lotions, and other new products that they'll be happy to hand out.

Peelies

Peelies are a type of coupon that all of us have seen and almost all of us have tossed in the trash. They are found directly on individual products and are meant for use on that product.

Here's the thing about peelies: a peelie is meant for the person who is actually *buying* the product. If you don't buy the product, then you don't get the coupon. It's important to use these sales in the way they were intended and be considerate of other shoppers. There is nothing more frustrating than picking up a product off the shelf and seeing that shiny rectangle where your peelie is supposed to be. Around here we call 'em "peelie stealers"! Not buying the product? Then leave the peelie.

Special Displays

Ever walk through the store and see a big cardboard display set up? You know the kind. They are often stocked with soft drinks or chips, although they can be for just about any product. Displays like these are an awesome place to find coupons. You may have to hunt for them—but that's all part of the fun!

E-coupons

At first glance you may think that e-coupons and printables are the same thing. Not in the least. The word "e-coupon" is just the fancy couponer way of saying electronic coupon. These are the coupons some stores allow you to add directly onto your store loyalty card. No printing or clipping required! All you have to do is register with the store website, add in your loyalty card number, and scroll through the available offers. You get to choose which offers you want loaded to your card and they will be redeemed automatically at checkout.

Catalinas

Catalinas are a special kind of coupon that prints out of a machine after you have checked out. Sound familiar? Yep, that long strip of paper your cashier hands you along with your receipt. Those would be Catalinas. The interesting thing about Catalinas is that there are a couple of different ways to get them.

By Formula

Stores will often run deals where buying a certain product or a certain number of products will trigger specific Catalinas to print. This is where the formula comes into play. If you buy the right items, then you get the coupon. For example, if you buy three boxes of Betty Crocker Fruit Snacks in one transaction, the formula is set up to give you a Catalina for $2.00 off your next purchase of anything in the store.

By Shopping Habits

You may notice that you often get coupons for items you buy all the time, especially if your store has a loyalty card. So if you buy baby food, then don't be surprised when baby food coupons come flying out of the Catalina machine before you walk out the door.

By Purchasing a Competing Product

The last type of Catalina triggers after you buy a competing product. For example, buying Keebler cookies could get you a Nabisco coupon. Nabisco figures if you like cookies, you are the perfect buyer for their brand instead of the competitor's brand.

How do you find out what to buy? At Time 2 $ave we always make sure to tell you what to look for and what Catalinas are running in your favorite stores. You can also find out by checking the blog or website for your favorite store or with a quick trip to the customer service counter. Just make sure to check whether your Catalinas are store or manufacturer coupons because they can print out either way.

Blinkies

As you stroll down the grocery store aisle you might notice little boxes mounted on the shelves calling to you with a small red blinking light. These are blinkies. When you walk up to them there is usually a coupon sticking out. Snag the coupon and another one just like it will pop out in a few seconds.

Blinkies have a special place in my heart. Not only do they pop up in the craziest spots, but they manage to keep my children entertained as we walk through the store. They love scoping out the "tickets" and seeing who can come out of the store with the most. Plus, one of my best couponing stories is all about blinkies.

I was at the grocery store and the trip started out normally enough. I always make a point to keep my eyes peeled for new blinkies, tear pads, hang tags, or anything else that pops up. Well, this store happened to have an awesome blinkie coupon for $0.35 off brand-name veggies. Those same veggies were on BOGO sale at a different grocery store down the street, and that store doubled coupons. BOGO sale price? $0.70. Coupon value? $0.35. Price after doubled coupon? FREE cans of veggies!

Can you guess that I was excited? Even so, I always feel that it's important to think of other shoppers. The manufacturer and/or store never intended a sale or coupon to only benefit one person. For that reason I always say "take two the Time 2 $ave way." We want to share the love after all. With that in mind I grabbed my two coupons and headed for the checkout.

After piling all my items on the belt I realized I had left the store coupons I needed at home. Since I had formed a close relationship with the cashiers, they let me run home and bring them back. I only live about twelve minutes round-trip, so I dashed home, grabbed what I needed, and took off back to the store.

Walking back through the doors I thought to myself, *Well, as long as I'm here I think I'll get two more blinkies for the veggies.* I go to the shelf all excited about getting more free veggies and the blinkie machine is gone. Poof! Empty shelf. What in the world happened? I was just here twelve minutes ago!

I looked around, thinking someone had swiped it, when I saw a lady in the same aisle. She had a screwdriver in her hand and was dismantling the blinkie machine with it! My mind raced—was she planning a fast getaway with the beloved blinkies? Surely no one would actually steal a blinkie machine?

By now I think you all know that *shy* isn't a word that describes me. So what did I do? I marched myself down the aisle to ask her, kindly, what she was doing. I don't know what I expected, but I didn't expect her to turn around with the sweetest smile in the world and say, "I'm the blinkie lady. I'm changing out the coupons."

Um . . . what? There's a blinkie lady? Really? Who knew?

Up until that moment I always thought the store put these things out, but as it happens a company called Smart Source (the same one that puts out the weekly inserts) handles the disbursement and changing out of the coupons. We chatted for a few minutes and I told her all about how I couponed and how I was able to use it to save so much money. She was more than a little surprised that the coupons she had been installing in blinkie machines in grocery stores were really that valuable. She then continued to tell me that no one really used all that many as she opened her little garbage bag and said, "Look, there are probably fifty coupons here that I just dumped out of that blinkie machine. Do you want them?"

Is it bad that I had to contain myself so I didn't attack her right then and there? It was all I could do not to grab the bag and run! Instead, I managed to say calmly, "Why, I'd hate for you to throw them away. If you don't have any use for them, then I would be happy to take them off your hands." Inside my head it sounded more like, "WOOOO-HOOOOOO!!! YES!"

She handed over the coveted coupon stash and on the way home I swung by the other store to pick up ten free cans of yummy veggies. Why ten? This store's policy is to only double ten like coupons at a time. And I knew this by asking at the customer service counter. I shared some of those coupons, stocked my pantry, and donated several cans of veggies to others. By the way, Teresa Graham? I will forever be indebted to you for being so kind to this girl who was acting like a crazy coupon lady.

(Disclaimer: I understand my story here kind of contradicts itself in regards to "take two the Time 2 $ave way" since when I returned to the store I was headed for two more coupons. I don't do that now; way back when, the blinkie lady just dumped fifty blinkies in the garbage. Nowadays a blinkie machine is lucky to last two days before running out. Just sayin' . . .)

Tear Pads

Tear pads are small pads of coupons usually stuck to a shelf or display. The cool thing about tear pads is they tend to pop up all over the place, not just in your favorite grocery store. Have a favorite soft drink? Then make sure you scan the shelf the next time you stop by a convenience store. It doesn't happen every day, but you just might find a great coupon that you can't find anywhere else.

Like blinkies, tear pads are on the honor system. When you find one you don't yank the whole thing off the shelf. You take two, and only two, and leave the others for someone else. Restraint is a good thing. Plus, you wouldn't want to be the one staring at the bare tear pad that someone else has just emptied with one swipe.

Printables

Whereas yesterday's shoppers were limited to coupons that came out of the newspaper, today's shoppers can find coupons for just about any item without looking further than their own computer. The first thing to know about printables is that each coupon comes with a print limit, which is usually two. Sometimes you will find the odd coupon that can be printed as many times as you want, but that is definitely more the exception than the rule.

Once the print limit is reached, that's it. Keep in mind, it's considered coupon fraud to copy coupons. Each internet printable is uniquely coded, and it can be traced back to your computer's IP address. Playing by the rules is always the best choice.

Where do you find great printables? While there are several places, just stop by Time 2 $ave before you go scouring the internet. We link each store ad directly to any printables you might want to use. These links will take you to places like:

- Coupons.com
- SmartSource.com
- RedPlum.com
- Couponnetwork.com
- Target.com
- Facebook.com

One more thing about printables: you need to watch the calendar. Each month most of the companies listed above put out a brand-new crop of printable offers. But these new coupons come standard with a print limit, so if there is one you know you want, make sure to print it early. If you wait too long, then it might just be gone. The early bird catches the worm with printables for popular items. This is the case more and more as couponing gains popularity and printable coupons hit their preset limits more quickly. Often we alert readers to a new coupon in the morning and by evening it's gone!

Also, print limits are tied to your computer's IP address. So if you have access to more than one computer then you can increase your savings.

Product Packaging

Ever check out the inside of a cereal box? Most of us don't. But if you did you might notice that sometimes you can find coupons printed right on the cardboard. And it's not limited to just cereal. Many products use their packaging to offer additional savings to their customers. Think of it as an enticement to buy more. Always check the box before it makes its way to the trash.

Manufacturers

Sometimes when you need an answer you've got to go straight to the horse's mouth. In the case of coupons that means the manufacturer. If you have a favorite item that you can never find a coupon for, don't be afraid to call or write to the manufacturer and ask about it. It doesn't always work, but you can sometimes find great savings that don't exist anywhere else.

The best way to ask for coupons is to tell the manufacturer how much you love the product they put out. (You catch more flies with honey!) Here's an example: "Hey! My family loves Product X and I'd love to know if you have any coupons available!" Simple, truthful, and often highly effective.

A System That Works . . . for You!

So what happens once you collect your coupons? Where do you put them? Do you pile them haphazardly on top of your desk? Or stuff them in a large envelope? Maybe you neatly tuck them away in a cute little coupon tin. Or maybe you are one of the holdouts who still goes for the ever popular inside pocket of your purse. After all, this has worked *so* well for you in the past.

Today we are going to put those purse stuffing days far behind us as we look at a better way to clip, sort, and store coupons. I'm going to walk you through how to organize your coupons based on what has worked for me and for thousands of people who have attended the Time 2 $ave workshops.

Step 1: Sorting

Let's take this step-by-step. For the sake of simplicity we are going to say that we buy five newspapers every week.

- Start by taking all of your newspapers for the week and pulling out the coupon inserts. The number of inserts will vary by week, so make sure you look carefully and don't miss anything.

- Next, separate your inserts into like piles: Smart Source, Red Plum, Proctor & Gamble, and so forth.

- Now you are going to need some space. Choose one type of insert to start with—say, Smart Source—and spread it open. Lift each page out, starting a pile for page 1, a pile for page 2, and so on. Continue pulling out pages and putting them into their correct piles until you have gone through all Smart Source inserts. When you are done, each pile will contain like pages. For example, I get five newspapers, so if the Smart Source insert had eight pages, I will now have eight piles of five.

- Grab your stapler! You want to staple each coupon right on the picture if you can. This may seem strange, but by stapling *before* you cut your stacks, your coupons will stay firmly together. They won't slip and slide while cutting and you won't end up with important barcodes getting snipped off.

- Repeat this process until you have all your inserts sorted and stapled. You are ready to clip.

Now when you get to the checkout counter you just pull the number of coupons you want to use off the stapled stack. You've basically created your own tear pad. It's a great trick! As I pointed out earlier, you don't want to staple the words because they might tear a bit when you pull the staple out.

I would love to say the idea of stapling came to me in a moment of organizational genius, but we all know that didn't happen. No, it came about more from my attempt to get out of cutting coupons altogether.

Let me explain. Okay, so you all know that I get multiple newspapers every week. Yeah, well what I'm about to tell you took me over a year to figure out. I discovered that instead of cutting each insert separately, if I joined like pages together then I could cut out all my coupons at the same time. Previously I would cut each insert on its own and end up with a huge pile of coupons that would take the better part of a day to sort through. Now I only had to cut once. Hallelujah!

Then, I had another great idea. I started hearing how several of my friends let their young daughters cut out their inserts for them—the angels started to sing for a second time! I was about to be set free from the clipping duty and I could see the light at the end of the tunnel. I just had to convince my daughter that this would be an *amazing* thing for her to get to do every week.

I started out by asking if she wanted to help me, making a big deal about it the whole time. This was going to be fun! I really tried to hype it up, because she's a lot like her momma and I know that sitting still is a serious challenge for her. So we sat down at the table and I carefully separated each set of like inserts, stacking the pages perfectly to make sure they were all lined up. Remember, I was trying to make this *fun*! I wanted it to be exciting for her so she would fall in love with cutting out coupons, thus relieving me from the task.

We each grabbed scissors and started cutting. I thought things were going pretty well until I noticed that expiration dates were missing, coupons were being cut out sideways—you name it. First, the problem was that her attention span only lasted through about the first three coupons. Second, it was just too difficult for her to keep all the pages lined up.

She thought she was free forever when I snatched up the stapler and quickly stapled each coupon without really thinking about it. Now I didn't have to worry about her keeping the pages together! It wasn't until a bit later that I realized the true genius of my new trick. I mean, now all the coupons stayed together *and* they fit better in my binder.

I know that my daughter will never *love* clipping coupons. But she is willing to help and we both enjoy having our M&M time: Morgan & Mommy!

Step 2: Clipping

When I first started couponing I spent far too much time sorting and clipping my coupons. It felt like a never-ending process. For my own sanity, I knew that there *had* to be a better way. And I found it. Now you get the benefit of skipping the madness and going straight to the easy breezy.

The first part to this new system is stapling. The second part comes into play during clipping. My goal is to only touch each coupon twice. To help achieve this goal I have fourteen little bins or tubs I lay out in front of me while I clip. Each tub is labeled with the same categories I have in my binder. This saves a ton of time because I literally hold the coupon over the appropriate bin when I am cutting so that it lands right there with its brothers and sisters. This way when I finish cutting I don't have a huge pile of coupons strewn all over my family room. Instead, all of the coupons are already separated into the appropriate categories.

If I don't feel like filing right now, I don't. I simply stack up my tubs and put them away. Otherwise I would have the biggest mess in all creation. Plus, I don't know about your kids, but I haven't met a kid yet who isn't magnetically attracted to coupons. No matter how carefully I planned where to hide my stacks, someone would always walk straight through the middle of them. Now if worse comes to worst, I just stack up my tubs and haul them to the store with me.

Are you shocked? You know you aren't! And you know I don't feel bad about it either. Remember, it's all about life and what we can fit into a day. If I don't have the time to neatly file my coupons, then I don't have the time. I'm still going to go to the store. Couponing is not going to take over my life or take me away from time with my family. So my biggest piece of advice is not to stress about your organizational method. Whatever you choose to use, it doesn't have to be perfect. It just has to work for you.

Looking at Options

Now that you are a sorting and clipping couponing pro, let's talk about organizing. I know, it's a dirty word to me too. But we can do it! The trick is finding what works for you. It's not a one-size-fits-all kind of thing.

I'm going to lay out three options. Each one works and each one is simple in its own way. It may be that one of these choices fits you to a T. If so, perfect. Or it may be that you want to take a little bit of this and throw in a little bit of that to come up with something uniquely you. That's great too. Feel free to mix and match to your heart's content. Seriously, there are no rules here other than you need a system that you can work with. Period.

The Binder Option

As the binder option is probably the most popular choice, we'll start there. It's straightforward and works great, especially for newbies and an untold number of ten-year-old boys who still treasure their baseball cards.

As you might have guessed, you start with a binder. Some people prefer the ones that zip shut, others like a nice heavy three-ring, but all that really matters is that it works for you.

Next, you're going to need a couple sets of dividers and the secret ingredient: several packs of baseball card holders. Baseball card holders are clear 8.5 x 11 sheets that boast a total of sixteen pockets per sheet. Each one of these little pockets can be used to file coupons, making them easy to store, see, and locate when you need them. Now, sit down and think about coupon categories that make sense to you. Picture the layout of your grocery store and make categories for each section of your binder such as "Canned & Boxed Items," "Breakfast," "Personal Care," "Cleaning Products," "Refrigerated," "Frozen," and "Pets." You get the picture. You can go for as many as you like; that's the beauty of coming up with your own system.

Once you have your list made out, label your section dividers, put your binder together, and start filing. It's that easy. You have all your coupons in one place ready for you to grab as you walk out the door. A word to the wise: if you choose to use a binder that does not zip shut, then always take care to hold it right side up. Not doing so has the potential to end in a confetti shower that you will *not* appreciate.

The Filing System

Have a great old box or basket hanging around? Then you already have the basics for creating your very own filing system. The great part is that you can use anything from a cardboard shoebox to a recipe box, a plastic tub with a lid, or even a tackle box. You can go big or small, it really doesn't matter. All that matters is that the size works for you.

Here's how it works. Start by buying or making dividers that fit the size of your box. Dividers are pretty easy to make out of index cards, cardstock, or even cardboard boxes. Then, just like with the binder system, label the dividers based on the categories that make sense to you. Now all that's left is to file your clipped coupons away.

The great part of this system is that it's super portable. With all your coupons in one place like this, you just have to grab your box and head to the store. The downside is that it can be time consuming to continually have to flip through the categories to find what you want. But if that doesn't deter you, then give it a try. It might turn out to be the perfect fit!

Whole-Insert Filing Option

This system is quick and easy and great for those of you who avoid clipping coupons like the plague. Although I used a binder system for years, I have recently switched to this method to save time. With this system you store your inserts whole, only clipping the coupons you plan to use each week. The idea is simple, and it works well for many people. Basically, it looks something like this.

Start by getting a file box, the kind you can store hanging files in. You will need the box, a pack of hanging files, a black Sharpie, and some file folders. Once you have your supplies together, it's time to add the coupons!

I would recommend sorting and stapling the inserts just like we have already talked about. Then, with your Sharpie, write the date it ran on the front of each insert. So an insert you found in the February 11 Sunday paper would be labeled "2/11." All of the inserts from the same date will be slipped into a folder and placed in one of the hanging files. Repeat this process each week, moving toward the back of the box chronologically. (Look on the insert's spine to find the date it ran. This is a great help if you've mixed them up and you're not sure what's what.)

The upside to this system is that it works well with the way we do matchups at Time 2 $ave. If a matchup says you'll need the coupon from the 2/11 Red Plum, all you have to do is flip to the 2/11 folder and look in the Red Plum insert to see if you have the coupon. It is also fairly quick and doesn't require you to clip every single coupon.

The downside is that unless you want to carry around a huge file box and a pair of scissors, you can't take all your coupons to the store with you. So if you come across a deal you weren't expecting (like a clearance

5 Tips for Couponing with Kids

- Cut out pictures of items you are purchasing from the weekly circular. Grab glue and paper and let your little one make their own grocery list. Once you are in the store have them keep their eyes open for those items.

- Teach your kids how to cut out coupons, and set aside expired ones to send overseas to military families.

- Depending on your child's age, practice math skills. For example, "Can you count how many boxes of spaghetti noodles? 1, 2, 3!" Older children can add up the cost of items to keep a running total or figure out the final cost of an item after coupons.

- Pay older kids a commission to keep your coupons organized and ready for a shopping trip. Pay them a percentage of how much you saved.

- Pick a donation item together each time you go to the grocery store. Become purposeful givers.

deal), then you are pretty much out of luck. Also, when you file like this it is harder to get a good sense of what coupons you have in the first place. Clipping, while time consuming, gives you the chance to look at each coupon and gives you an idea of what you have to work with.

Choosing What Works

All of these systems work. We know that. But they may not work for *you*. And that's okay! It's about finding what makes your life easier.

And if it's not one of these systems, that's fine. Just look at this as a starting point. All I ask is that you try something, because you don't want to go back to being the girl with a pocketful of coupons hidden down in her purse. We all know how that one ends.

ACTION STEP
Go on a scavenger hunt.

Go on a scavenger hunt in your store and find three new places where coupons hide that you haven't seen before. It's all about keeping your eyes peeled! Look for tear pads, blinkies, peelies, and every other type of coupon we've talked about. This fun little exercise will help you get used to looking for coupons and will greatly expand your coupon stash.

ACTION STEP
Decide how you want to organize your coupons.

At this point, go ahead and decide how you'd like to organize your coupons. (Remember, you can change your mind later.)

In this chapter we have talked about three different organizational methods:

1. Staple, clip, and file in a binder
2. Staple, clip, and file in a box or basket
3. Date and file whole, unclipped inserts

If you choose option 1 or 2, you'll need to create categories to file your coupons under. Sit down and think of how your grocery store is laid out. Make a list of categories. (You can see a sample category list in appendix E.) By organizing your coupons under these categories, you'll easily be able to pull out what you need when you're in any given aisle of the grocery store. Also this week, make a trip to pick up coupon supplies. Pick up two Sunday papers to start with, as well as a binder (and baseball card holders to fill it with) or baskets. Another handy item to get is a pack of sticky tabs to write your categories on.

Categorize your binder or baskets using your sticky tabs or dividers. Then, using the steps described in this chapter, clip and file away this week's coupons.

If you choose option 3, simply write this Sunday's date on the front page of each insert using a Sharpie and slip it into a file box.

6

Ready . . . Set . . . Shop!

So what now? You've learned to decode the lingo. You know how to read a store matchup. You can even spot a tear pad hiding two aisles away. And now you are wondering how it all comes together. In fact, the question I get asked most often is simply, "What now?" Well, it's kind of like driving a car. You can read all the books you want and study all the technical data under the sun, but it takes actually sliding behind the wheel to learn how to drive.

With that in mind, it's time to do one of your favorite things—shop! Okay, it may not be your favorite yet, but once you go in armed with all of the tricks, tips, and tools you're learning, it will be. Just think how you'll feel that first time you walk out of the store having saved as much as 50 percent off your bill. You're going to do a happy dance right there in the parking lot.

Now, back to driving. By the time we are old enough to drive we've already spent the better part of our life riding around in cars. We know how to stop at stop signs, we know what a red light looks like, we know what the blinker is for, and we even know how to check the rearview mirror. We understand the basics. The problem is that watching someone else drive doesn't teach you how to do it. Watching only teaches you *about* driving, and up to this point I've only taught you *about* couponing. It's going to take you actually walking into a store and giving it a try to learn *how* to coupon. My goal is to help you prepare. I want you to know everything you possibly can about couponing so that when you are ready to jump in all you have to concentrate on is the how.

In this chapter we are going to look at how to read the weekly circulars and pick out the best deals. Then we will take that knowledge and check out three different ways to plan your shopping trip from beginning to end. I'll teach you how to collect and print coupons to go along with your grocery list, which will include both your "must-haves" and "stockpile items." I'll also show you how to shop for things to grow your stockpile week by week.

To help you really see what it looks like to get your list together, this chapter will also walk you through the weekly deal matchups from the Time 2 $ave blog. (Want to try it right now? Visit www.time2save workshops.com and click "Get Store Deals" in the top right corner.) I want to make it as easy as possible to fit couponing into your life. It doesn't have to eat up every spare (or not so spare) moment. So take advantage of the shortcuts on Time 2 $ave and get ready to shop!

A-Shopping We Will Go!

So what's the first step in getting ready for your inaugural coupon shopping trip? Well, for starters you're going to need a list, one that groups items into two categories: stockpile items and must-haves. The stockpile items are those things your family uses that are at their absolute rock-bottom price. You'll buy more of these items because you want to have some to use now and some to add to your stockpile. The must-haves are pretty self-explanatory. These are the items that will send you back to the store tomorrow if you come home without them today. For example, if you're out of toilet paper and come home empty-handed, then someone is heading back out before things get a little more real than anyone wants to deal with!

At the beginning, you will have many must-haves on your list; that's totally normal. But over time you will start to see a shift in your grocery list. As you build your pantry week after week, items will fall off your must-have list until the balance moves away from *need* and into *use*. In others words, you'll stop having to buy so many must-haves because the stockpile items have knocked them off your list.

One Example

This week toilet paper is on your must-have list, and since there isn't a great deal on it, you just have to bite the bullet and buy some. Next week, however, you find a great sale on toilet paper, plus you have some coupons for it, and combined they make for a rock-bottom price. Since this is the best price you have seen, you buy several packages—which go into your stockpile. Now toilet paper is knocked off your list and won't make its way back to the must-have column for several weeks. Long enough for you to sit back and wait for another spectacular deal.

The graph below will give you a better idea of what I'm talking about. Keep in mind that this process takes time. You can't build a pantry overnight.

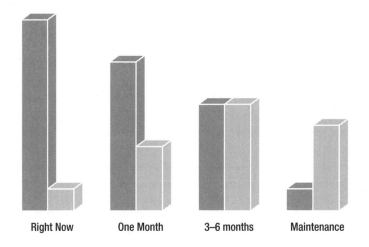

| Right Now | One Month | 3–6 months | Maintenance |

In the graph above, the dark bars represent your must-have items, and the light bars represent your stockpile items. At this point you haven't started or maybe you have just started building your stockpile. This means you are still going to have to pay full price for many of the items your family needs. The key to building your pantry is to set aside $5 to $10 per week to use on stockpile items. That might not seem like a lot of money, but when you are purchasing items as cheaply as possible you'll be amazed at how far it will go.

Where to Start

These three steps deal with assessing your needs and your available coupons.

Step 1: Make a list of the items you *need*. I know you have just learned how to stop shopping out of need, but you can't start at the top. Until your pantry begins to fill up with everyday items, they won't be disappearing off your list.

Step 2: Check your coupons. Do you have any coupons for the items you need? They may not be on sale, but there's no reason not to save money everywhere you can. If you're not sure what coupons are floating around out there, then stop by the Time 2 $ave blog. Click on "Search Coupons" in the upper right corner to access our amazing coupon database that shows every available coupon for a given item.

Let's check out a few quick examples.

Example 1: Scott Bath Tissue

In this example we are looking at Scott Bath Tissue. (Really it's toilet paper. I mean, bath tissue? Just sounds silly to me!) We start by typing the product name into the search field. If you wanted to look for a different product, you would simply type the product name into the database and the program would show you what coupons are available for that product. Or if you really don't care what brand you use and just want to know the best options, type in "bath tissue or toilet paper."

In this case the database tells us there are two coupons available for Scott Bath Tissue. They include:

- $1 off an 8-pack of Scott Extra Soft Bath Tissue, found in the 1/15 Smart Source insert
- $0.55 off one 12-pack of Scott Bath Tissue, printable (the link is active so you simply click to be directed to print that coupon)

This example shows us a couple of things. First, you can usually find coupons for items even if they aren't on sale. Again, savings are savings no matter how small. Second, printable coupons are a great option when you are just starting out. It will take a few weeks for you to accumulate coupon inserts from the weekly paper, but that doesn't mean you can't coupon during that time. Printables like these show up frequently and are a great way to snag savings.

As you look through these examples, pay close attention to the description and requirements for each coupon. The first coupon is for a specific type and size of Scott toilet paper while the second is for any 12-pack Scott Bath Tissue.

Example 2: Kraft Salad Dressing

In this example, four coupons are available for this product:

- $0.75 off two 14 oz. Kraft Dressings, found in 1/22 Smart Source insert
- $1 off 2 Kraft Italian, Target Store printable coupon
- $1 off 2 Kraft Salad Dressing, Target Store printable coupon
- $1 off 2 Kraft Dressing, found in 1/22 Smart Source insert

A quick note about the last coupon listed in the example above: this is a great example of a regional variation. This coupon came out the same day and in the same insert as the first option listed. However, the values were very different. The coupon you receive would depend on the region where you live. You might receive one or the other or possibly even none at all, but just know that it is out of the newspaper's control. Remember that the largest paper in your area will have the best coupons.

Step 3: Once the must-haves are taken care of, we get to move on to the stockpile items. This is the fun part.

Start by writing down five meals your family loves. This way you can look for stockpile items to keep on hand for weekly meal planning. If you're on the Time 2 $ave website, look at the grocery matchups for your favorite stores. If you're not using the site, then find out what day your stores put out their new circulars and swing by to pick one up or visit their website to view it online.

But don't go overboard. As tempting as it will be to jump right in and tackle every store in your neighborhood, just pick one. No need to overload yourself with stores to hit each week. Figure out which store has the most items your family uses on sale this week. That's your winner!

Now let's figure out how many of each stockpile item you need to purchase. For each item on your sale list that your family uses, you have to ask yourself two questions:

- How much do you think your family will *use* over the next twelve weeks? (Don't stress if you aren't sure; this isn't an exact science.)
- How many coupons do you have?

Once you have the answers to these questions you can decide how many you want to purchase. For example, say Ritz Crackers are on BOGO sale for $1.69 and you have five $0.50/1 coupons. With these coupons you can purchase five boxes at $0.69 each if your store doubles. This is what we'd consider a rock-bottom price—just about as low as you can get, considering the store has cut the price in half and you've added a coupon to each item as well. Perfect for stockpiling! If you're happy with the $1.69 price, feel free to grab a couple extra even though you don't have the coupons. It's still a good deal and you will still get some great savings—so don't feel completely trapped by the number of coupons you have.

Hit the Ground Shopping

There are basically three different options for building your weekly shopping list. If you suddenly feel all panicky and overwhelmed, hear me out. I'm simply giving you options. Most of you will never have to worry about creating your own grocery matchup. At the same time, if you live in a more rural area and can't find your grocery store matchups online, it won't stop you from being able to coupon. It's important that you understand the process. In addition, none of us are immune to computer problems; if your computer crashes one week it doesn't mean you have to break your bank. Again, it's all about options:

- Matching your coupons to weekly circulars
- Matching your coupons to weekly circulars using the Time 2 $ave database
- Using the Time 2 $ave grocery and drugstore matchups

It doesn't matter which one you choose; like everything else with couponing, it only matters that you find a system that works for you.

Circular Matchup

Some couponers only like to look at deals they can get, meaning they are only interested in working with the coupons they have on hand. In this case the circular matchup method may be just your speed. This is also a great alternative for those who don't have access to a computer or aren't very tech savvy. Then there are those everyday nuisances that we can't prevent no matter how technologically advanced we are. Chances are at some point we'll all find ourselves with a printer or computer (or both) that crash. If that's the case, follow the steps outlined below. As I said before, it's important to have options.

Here's how it works: start with the coupons you have handy and the weekly circular from your favorite store. Take the circular one page at a time, comparing the sale items that your family uses and needs to the coupons you have on hand to see what matches up. As you go through each sale item, simply turn to the appropriate category in your binder or coupon box and scan through the coupons. As you find coupons that match sale items, go ahead and pull them out and set them aside. This method does take time, but the savings will still be worth it. The upside about using this method is that it does not require a computer at any point, meaning you can do it wherever you are. So if you have to wait for your kids at a weekly soccer game or dance practice where you usually sit twiddling your thumbs, that might be a great time to put this method to good use.

(Note: I would not recommend using the whole-insert filing method that we referred to in chapter 5 to organize your coupons if you choose to do the matchups yourself. In this case the binder or filing method would serve you much better.)

Database Matchup

The coupon database on the Time 2 $ave website is a great resource. It allows you to search the items on your list to find out what coupons are available and how they match up with the weekly sales at your favorite store.

Here's how it works. Refer to the circular from your favorite store and head over to the coupon database at the Time 2 $ave blog. Now, work your way through each item your family uses (or needs . . . remember, you are just getting started). Simply type each item in the search box, then click "search," and every available coupon for that item pops up. (We just covered this in detail a few pages back.) If the coupon is from an insert, go ahead and pull that coupon from your file and set aside. As a reminder, coupons are regional. If you can't find the coupon from a particular insert, then most likely your region didn't receive that coupon. Continue searching the database to find coupons to match the sale items in the circular.

Compare the sale items to see which ones match up to make the best deals. It takes some time, but this method will give you a great feel for what coupons are out there and help you become accustomed to working with the weekly circulars. Most importantly, it puts you in the driver's seat. If you can't find matchups for your favorite store online, it doesn't mean you can't coupon.

Using the Time 2 $ave Grocery and Drugstore Matchups

Go to the Time 2 $ave website, click on "Store Savings," and let us do the work for you. Each week we post the best deals for many major grocery chains and drugstores along with the coupons that match each item. All you have to do is pick your store from the list, scroll through the matchups, and pick out the items your family uses. At the end of this chapter I'll walk you step-by-step through the process of creating your customized grocery list.

Choose which option works best for you and jump in!

We've just covered all of the different options to start the process of pulling together a shopping trip. Now, let's go for a test drive.

Time for a Time 2 $ave Test Drive

Step 1: Go Online!

It's time to stop by Time 2 $ave and build your first couponing grocery list. Before you do, let's take a moment and make sure you are comfortable with the format we use on the blog. The goal here is to review a few matchups and make sure that you understand the lingo and how these lists break down. The following example is from a weekly Publix ad. Remember, Publix doubles manufacturer coupons up to $0.50 and accepts competitor coupons, so we're able to stack a manufacturer coupon with a competitor coupon in these examples.

Wish-Bone Dressing—$1.32
Use (2) $0.50/1, $0.70/1, or $0.65/2 from 1/29 RP
Stack with $0.50/2 Target PRINT
(makes it as low as $0.14 for 2 or $0.07 ea. wyb 2)

In this example there are three coupons listed for Wish-Bone Salad Dressing and they are all from the 1/29 Red Plum insert. What does this mean? It means that you are looking at another example of regional coupon variations. You could have any combination of the coupons listed or none at all depending on where you live.

Take a look at the last line in the example. On our blog this line is almost always listed in pink, and reads "makes it as low as." This tells you the lowest possible price based on the *best* coupons listed. In this case the $0.50/1 was doubled and then stacked with the Target store coupons to make the final cost $0.14 for two or $0.07 each. Not bad!

Examples using other coupons listed:

Wish-Bone Dressing—$1.32
Use $0.65/2 or $0.70/1 from 1/29 RP
Stack with $0.50/2 Target PRINT

In this example we would have to purchase two bottles since the coupon we are using is $0.65/2. Also, since Publix doubles coupons up to $0.50 this coupon will not double. Here are a few scenarios showing how this would break down.

Scenario 1:

Salad Dressing $1.32 x 2 (need 2 bottles) = $2.64
Use $0.65/2 from 1/29 RP
(makes it $1.99 for two or $0.99 each wyb 2)

Or

Salad Dressing $1.32 x 2 (need 2 bottles) = $2.64
Use $0.65/2 from 1/29 RP
Stack with $0.50/2 Target PRINT
(makes it $1.49 for two or $0.74 each wyb 2)

Scenario 2:

Salad Dressing $1.32 x 2 (need 2 bottles) = $2.64
Use (2) $0.70/1 from 1/29 RP
(makes it $1.24 for two or $0.62 each wyb 2)

Or

Salad Dressing $1.32 x 2 (need 2 bottles) = $2.64
Use (2) $0.70/1 from 1/29 RP
Stack with $0.50/2 Target PRINT
(makes it $0.74 for two or $0.37 each wyb 2)

These scenarios show that no matter which coupons you have, you are still going to see significant savings. Yes, some deals are better than others, but a deal is a deal! And there will be times when you have more than one of the coupons listed. Then you will have to look at your options and decide which one will make the best deal for the store where you are shopping.

Step 2: Where Are You Going?

In trying to decide which store to shop at, find the store that has the most items your family uses on sale that week. For example, based on the sales I'm about to share with you, this week I would choose to shop at Publix and forget about the other stores. Remember, our goal is not to run ourselves ragged trying to snag every bargain; it's to do the best with the time and resources that we have.

Here's what my list might look like this week at Publix versus BI-LO (keep in mind that Publix doubles coupons up to $0.50 and BI-LO doubles coupons up to $0.60):

Publix	BI-LO
Wish-Bone Dressing $1.32 Use $0.65/2, $0.50/1, $0.70/1 from 1/29 RP Stack with $0.50/2 Target PRINT (makes it as low as $0.07 ea. wyb 2)	Yoplait Greek Single Serve Yogurt $0.88 (limit 6) Use $0.50/2 from 1/25, 2/2 SS (makes it $0.38 ea. wyb 2)
Hall's Cough Drops $1.00 Use $0.50/1 from Feb. *All You* or $1/2 from 2/5 SS or $1/2 PRINT (makes it as low as FREE)	Birds Eye Voila! Dinner (21 to 23 oz.) $2.74 ea. Use $1.85/1 Birds Eye Voila! Product PRINT (makes it as low as $0.89)
Mt. Olive Sweet Relish or Pickles $1.20 Use $1/1, $0.75/1 from 1/22 SS (makes it as low as $0.20)	Scott Bath Tissue 8 Rolls $4.99 Use $0.55/1 Scott Tissue PRINT or $1/1 from 1/15 SS Stack $1/1 from Walgreens Feb. Coupon Booklet (makes it as low as $2.89!) *Limit 2
Mueller's Pasta $0.79 Use $1/2 from 1/8 SS (makes it $0.29 ea. wyb 2)	Hormel Deli meats (3.5 oz.) $1.49 ea. Use $0.50/1 from 1/8 SS or $1/2 from 1/15 SS or $0.55/2 PRINT (makes it as low as $0.49)
Green Giant Canned Vegetables $0.64 Use $1/4 PRINT (makes it as low as $0.39 ea. wyb 4)	

Step 3: What Do I Bring with Me?

Why, your list of course!

Before you head out, take a moment to sit back down at your computer (see step 1) and print out your very own customized shopping list from Time 2 $ave. (See the Publix and BI-LO lists above for an example.) You'll see a white box to the left of each item. All you do is check the boxes next to the items you want and then click on the "Create List" button at the bottom of the blog. This way you end up with a list that has everything you want and not a single thing that you don't. It's kind of like looking at a map that only shows you the places you want to go so everything else isn't distracting you.

Next, using your newly created list as a guide, grab your binder or file box and pull out any coupons you need before you go to the store. Also, this is the time to print any printable coupons, cut them out, and put them with your other coupons.

How should you do this? Well, let's look at that for a minute.

Binder

The first item on your list is the Wish-Bone Salad Dressing. Find the tab in your binder that correlates with that item (perhaps your tab is labeled "Condiments") and flip to it. Once you find what you are looking for, just pull it out and set it beside your list. Then move on to the next item.

Box or Basket

If you are using the box method, then go to the appropriate tabbed section and thumb through the coupons until you find the one you are looking for. Again, pull it out and set it aside with the rest of your list.

Whole Insert Filing Option

For the file box method you will need to note the date of each coupon you are looking for. In the example of the Wish-Bone Salad Dressing that would be the 1/29 Red Plum. This means you would go to the file dated 1/29 and pull out the Red Plum insert. Thumb through the insert to locate the coupon(s) you want. If you don't see it, then check the file to see if there was more than one Red Plum insert that week. If so, then look through the second insert. When you find what you are looking for, simply cut out the coupons you want and put the rest back into the file box. (If you still don't see it, most likely it is a regional variation that your area didn't get.)

Whichever method you use, you will repeat these steps for each item on your list. If you don't find a particular coupon, again it's probably a regional variation that was not distributed in your market.

Now I want to share a few quick tips that it took me a long time to figure out. See, in a perfect world clicking on a printable coupon would mean watching that coupon come gliding out of your printer. Unfortunately that isn't always the case. Here are a few things that can and do go wrong from time to time.

- The coupon may have reached its print limit. That limit is set by the manufacturer, and they go fast!
- You may have already printed that coupon the maximum number of times that month.
- The coupon was part of a promotion, and the promotion has ended.

I don't mention these things to discourage you. I'm only telling you this because I've been there. I have been standing in front of my printer convinced that my computer had a sick sense of humor about printing coupons. It just waited until it knew there was one I *really* wanted and then *refused* to send it sliding out of the printer. It is definitely a love/hate relationship that we have! As much as I was convinced that my computer was out to get me, it turns out that there are reasons coupons don't print. The ones listed above are the most common, but you will find a more complete list in appendix D if you have any questions. Now that you have your coupons clipped and your custom list printed out, you're almost ready to roll!

Step 4: Ready to Roll!

Here's my system for bringing my coupons to the store. After I have everything laid out I fold my list in half with my coupons inside. Then I put the whole bundle into an envelope. If I happen to be hitting more than one store that week (which is rare), then every bundle gets its own envelope and I make sure to label each one. It helps me keep everything together and remember which coupons go to which store.

Nothing fancy about it, but it gets the job done for me! You might do something totally different.

Are you ready to hop in the car? I bet you thought this moment would never come. Woo-hoooo! We've been prepping nonstop and it's finally time to put all these new skills to good use. Ladies and gentlemen, start your engines!

Remember your first attempt at driving? Did it feel as awkward for you as it did for me? I'm telling you, it scared the hound diggity out of me. I didn't think I'd ever learn how to keep that thing in the right lane. Shoot, the first time I set the wheels rolling I didn't even make it out of my grandparents' driveway before managing to back into the bushes. How in the world was I supposed to drive if I couldn't even get out of the driveway?

However, thinking back, my first driving experience actually happened years before I hit the bushes. I didn't know anything about how a car worked or the rules of the road. I didn't even know what the signs meant. I was only about four years old; my grandmother had gone into the doctor's office and I was sitting in the car with my great-grandmother. (Keep in mind, this was before car seats became law.) Before my great-grandmother could stop me I grabbed the gear-shift, pulled the car out of park, and sent it rolling backward.

Next thing I knew the car was rolling down the hill and all the way across the road to smack square into the florist shop on the other side of the street. Honey, I don't do anything halfway! That wall? It didn't stop the car. That would be too easy. No, we barreled right through the wall and ended up hanging out in the middle of a giant pile of squished posies. Luckily no one was hurt and my grandparents' car was fine. (Plus my grandfather was able to put the shop back together.) But all in all, my first trip was a disaster. I know, I was only four, but it's the concept that counts.

The moral of the story? If you try to coupon without understanding the process, I can guarantee you'll hit a wall and want to give up. The great news is you aren't four years old. You've put in the work and you're ready. So let's go to the store.

Hitting the Store

Since we are going to Publix this week, I'm going to walk you through what I would do on an average trip. First thing to do is get your list and coupons out. Before we get too far into the store, I want to share a quick note about binders and buggies. Unless grocery carts have been reengineered in the last few weeks, trying to prop your binder up in the buggy is going to drive you nuts. Save your sanity, grab your purse or some of your reusable shopping bags, and place it underneath your binder. If you don't, then the binder is going to flop back and forth since it's about an inch too short to stay where it needs to. You'll thank me later.

Next, head over to the customer service counter and see if they have any coupons. Take the bundle they offer, give it a quick glance just in case there is anything you want to use during today's trip, and then put the rest away so you can file them later.

As you walk through the aisles, tossing a little of this and a little of that into your buggy, you need to somehow separate out the coupons that you now plan to use. For example, say you have five coupons for the Wish-Bone Salad Dressing from the example above, but there are only three bottles left on the shelf. You will end up using three of your coupons and saving two for later.

I take the coupons I am going to use, turn them around backward, and put them in the very back of my envelope. This helps me keep all the coupons I'm going to use together in one place so they don't get lost by the time I check out.

Work your way through the store and through your list. Hopefully you will be able to find everything that you want, but if not, it's time for another trip to customer service, this time for rain checks. A rain check is a special slip issued by the store when they are out of a particular sale item. It allows you to take advantage of the sale price at a later date once the item is back in stock.

Rain checks have a special place in my heart. They're perfect for procrastinators like me. If there are items you still really want but the shelves are empty, then grab a rain check. Customer service will be happy to write them up for you; you just have to make sure not to lose them. Pick a spot in your binder or filing system just for rain checks. That way you always know where to look when you are ready to put them to good use.

Checkout Time

Okay, if you haven't organized the coupons you are going to use, then find a quiet spot to do so now. Go through and count your items to make sure you have the right number of coupons pulled out for each item on your list. Planning on stacking? Then you'll need those coupons too. It really helps to look everything over just one more time before you head to the checkout, mostly because you don't want to miss anything. I've had trips when I'm walking out the door looking at my receipt only to realize I forgot to use this coupon or that rain check.

Going through the line is the easy part, and it's the fun part! Just put your groceries up on the belt, hand over your coupons, and watch the total drop. With every little *beep* that number will get smaller and smaller as your smile gets bigger and bigger. You'll walk out of the store feeling lighter, happy, and hopefully more than a little excited.

Why? Because *you* are officially a couponer!

Top Five Couponing Myths Debunked

- **If there is a 10 for $10 sale, I've got to buy all ten items to get the sale price.**

  10 for $10 Sale—You don't always have to buy all ten to get the $1 per item price. Just look at the items as if they were all on sale for $1. Make sure to check with your local store to find out how they handle this type of sale.

- **You can only use store coupons at that specific store.**

  Nope! Some stores will allow you to use competitor coupons, which are store coupons from a competing store.

- **It's impossible to save money if the grocery stores in my area don't double coupons.**

  You can still save money even if none of the stores in your area double coupons. Don't let this discourage you from shopping with coupons; it doesn't mean that you won't be able to save tons of money. There are many other options, such as shopping at drugstores, that will afford you tremendous savings. Still not convinced? Think about it this way: what if there were two doors in front of you? You can see both Door A and Door B along with the contents behind each, yet you only have the option of choosing Door A. What do you do?

  Door A = $20 bill

  Door B = $100 bill

Do you say, "Keep the $20. If I can't have the $100 behind Door B I'm not playing"? I doubt it. Free money is free money. Of course I'd prefer the crisp $100 bill, just as I'd prefer to save $100 over $20. However, you won't catch me turning free money away. That $20 bill behind Door A has my name all over it. At the end of the day, whether I save $20 or $100, I'm still saving my family money.

- **I've heard that all of the couponers clear the shelves of sale items.**

  It is unlikely that every time you go to the store they will be out of all the items that you were planning on purchasing. There will be times when some items are out of stock, but that doesn't mean your opportunity to purchase these items is dependent upon the store's being fully stocked. The solution is simple: ask for a rain check. Then add those items to your shopping list next week.

- **I always spend more money when I shop with coupons, and we just can't afford it.**

  That could be true, but it doesn't have to be. Most people who have tried couponing at one time or another experienced the same thing. I know I did. However, there is a difference between couponing and couponing effectively. If you follow the steps I've outlined, I can assure you that your grocery bill will decrease dramatically. But it won't happen overnight. It's a process.

Remember, always refer to your store's coupon policy to clarify any questions you may have about it.

ACTION STEP

Make your first Time 2 $ave shopping list.

Go online and make a practice list on the Time 2 $ave blog. Choose the store you shop at most frequently and cruise through, looking closely at all the sales listed for the week. Now, find one product that *really* interests you and take this little six-question quiz to test your coupon matchup comprehension.

1. Of the options listed, which coupon is the best one to use on this product? (Remember, some stores will double coupons up to a certain amount.)

2. Where can you find the coupons listed? Are they printables? Or did they come from a newspaper, magazine, blinkie machine, or peelie?

3. If the coupon is from a newspaper insert, can you find it in the Red Plum, Smart Source, Proctor & Gamble, or General Mills insert?

4. If the coupon is from a newspaper insert, when was that insert released?

5. Is there a store or competitor coupon that can be stacked with the manufacturer coupon listed?

6. What will your final price be if you have the best coupons listed?

How did you do? Great! Now, check the boxes beside the items you'd like to buy and print out your very first shopping list!

7

Sensible Stockpiling

Don't store up treasures here on earth, where moths eat them and rust destroys them, and where thieves break in and steal. Store your treasures in heaven, where moths and rust cannot destroy, and thieves do not break in and steal. Wherever your treasure is, there the desires of your heart will also be.

Matthew 6:19–21

The Basics of Building a Sensible Stockpile: Having What You Need at Your Fingertips

I'm guessing that by this time many of you have seen the crazy photos of extreme couponers showing off their massive stockpiles. Yep, those things look pretty intimidating, don't they? I mean, even the word *stockpile* brings forth images of people out in their backyards building fallout shelters for a nuclear disaster. Either that, or they have rooms devoted to toilet paper storage or entire closets of toothpaste just waiting to clean the teeth of the next three generations.

This is *not* the kind of stockpile we're learning how to build in this chapter. Rather, it is about buying what we will need and use during the next three months. In other words, I want to have a well-stocked pantry, not hole up enough items to feed a family of twelve for the next five years. Shopping this way will save you money. It will also give you a way to shop from home so you only *have* to go to the grocery store for the fresh items you need to replenish quickly, like bread, milk, eggs, and produce.

I like to call this "sensible stockpiling." It's smart, practical, and doesn't involve going overboard.

It's very difficult to master the art of couponing without having a stocked pantry. One of our goals is to avoid as much as possible paying full price for the items we use. The only way to do this is to buy enough of an item while it's super cheap to last until the next sale cycle. It's a simple concept, and it has some impressive benefits.

For example, shopping this way will all but eliminate those one-item trips to the grocery store. You know the ones I'm talking about. Those days when you walk in looking to buy cheese for the tacos you're making for dinner and walk out with four full bags of groceries. This kind of trip costs you time and money.

Let me share what a good friend of mine has to say on the subject:

I used to be one of those people who said I couldn't possibly buy extra items . . . I could barely afford what I needed on a weekly basis, let alone buy extra. But I started stockpiling about five months ago, mostly on items I got from CVS sales—shampoo, toothpaste, razors, laundry detergent, dish detergent, and so forth. The best part is, after you get into it a few months and start to build your stockpile, you will notice you don't need nearly as much at the grocery store each week. And you can buy more and more items that are on sale with that extra money. It's a great feeling, when everyone is complaining about the cost of everything, to know you are actually paying less for things than you did a year ago, and if you had to, you could go for a while without buying anything! Stockpiling is the best.

See? The best! And you can do it too. In this chapter we are going to learn what it takes to build and organize your sensible stockpile. Plus, we'll find creative places to store your groceries and household items, learn how to be flexible with brand loyalties, and even talk about planning meals around your stockpile to avoid extra trips to the grocery store.

Let's see if this sounds familiar. It's 4:30 in the afternoon and I'm making lasagna for dinner. The best part? I've got everything I need. I've got all the ingredients, have the casserole put together, the salad is made, and I'm about two minutes from turning on the oven for the bread.

Wait . . . bread! How could I have forgotten that I don't have any bread? Oh well, I can at least go ahead and set the table, grab the salt and pepper, and pull out the salad dressing. Hmmmm . . . I thought I had a brand-new bottle of salad dressing. Where did that get to? Forget it! I'm out of time. I'll just run to the store and grab a bottle to go with the bread I now need. The lasagna is cooking and I can be back in less than ten minutes.

Then, I walk into the store and it's like my brain just disconnects from my body. I *planned* to grab the two items I needed and get back home before the timer dinged, but somehow two has turned into twenty. On my way to get the dressing I realize we need some juice. My husband and daughter are diabetic and we have to keep juice boxes with us all the time in case their blood sugar drops. It's not on sale, but we've got to have it. Oh look! My favorite cookies! Better grab a pack of those too. Hey, Powerade is 10 for $10! My kids love that stuff!

And so on and so on and so on, until I've managed to spend $75 on bread and salad dressing. Not only that, but I didn't even get a good deal on anything I bought. I forgot everything I had learned and fell back into that old habit of shopping for what my family needs instead of for what we use. Don't fall into this trap; plan ahead.

Our goal is to stock up on the items we need when they are at their lowest, rock-bottom price. In doing so we cross these items off our list until the next sale cycle and save ourselves from those "got to get it now" trips to the store. We want to maximize our coupon savings and get the best possible value for our money.

In the last chapter we walked through how to navigate the Time 2 $ave blog, build your list, and prepare for your trip. Now we are going to take those skills and use them to build a stockpile of the items your family uses every week.

Ready? Here we go!

Be Flexible with Brand Loyalties

One of the first things you can do as you get set to stockpile is change your mindset. Are you brand loyal? Yep, so was I until I found out I could purchase a different name-brand peanut butter for $0.40 a jar instead of $3.86. It doesn't mean you will like your new brand better, but this type of price difference will definitely make you open to trying something new.

If you only ever buy one certain brand of something, you're going to have to wait much longer for the opportunity to stockpile it. But if you work at stockpiling the item and not the brand (salad dressing, not Hidden Valley or Kraft or Wish-Bone), you will have so many more chances to get a great deal.

What Items Should You Buy for Your Stockpile?

Want to know what to buy for your stockpile? Then check out appendix B of this book! You will find a list of items you should look for when building your stockpile. Take this list and make it your own. Mark off the items you'll never use (in my house that would be mayonnaise and tuna . . . gross!). Consider your family's eating habits and fill your pantry accordingly. For example, if your family only goes through five boxes of cereal in a year, then this isn't an item you will need to focus on. But if you tend to use a full jar of peanut butter every week, then that is a sale you want to take advantage of.

Quick note: I still live by the principle of looking beyond the needs of my own family. For me this means actively searching for those items I can buy and donate each time I go to the grocery store. It might mean picking up a few extra boxes of cereal here and there or even sucking it up and buying mayonnaise that I know someone else would use. I'm not going to stock up on items I know we won't eat, but I will grab one or two to donate and then keep on walking.

With this in mind, approach the sale matchups each week looking for those items you want to stock up on. It's a process and it won't happen overnight, but with time your weekly grocery list will begin to shift from need to use as you stock your pantry and knock those must-have items off your list.

Over the next twelve weeks you will be purchasing different sale items each time you shop. Remember? It's about finding that rock-bottom price and taking advantage of it. Yes, you are buying enough to get through this sale cycle, but you aren't buying enough to last the rest of your life. For example, our goal is not to buy five hundred tubes of toothpaste so that we never have to buy it again. The idea is that you will begin to run low on specific items just as the next sale cycle rolls around.

Back in chapter 6 we talked about what your "list" would look like in a given week. Now we are going to look at that same list in relation to building your pantry.

This is where setting aside between $5 and $10 a week to build your pantry comes into play. I know it doesn't seem like much, but we can make that money stretch a looooong way! Some weeks you may only have one pantry item on your list, but don't let that discourage you. Those items will add up week after week until one day you open the door and find this wonderfully stocked pantry staring back at you.

Here is an example of a pantry stockpile list:

Items to Target

Cheese	Salad dressing	Veggies	Oatmeal
Rice	Crackers	Butter	Mustard
Pickles	Bread	Jelly	Pasta sauce
Chicken	Pasta	Cleaning wipes	Bleach
Shampoo	Detergent	Dryer sheets	Window cleaner
Toothpaste	Toilet paper	Paper towels	Furniture polish

Now let's look at what shopping for pantry items might look like.

Green Giant Vegetables—$0.64 ea. or $1.28 BOGO
Use $1/4 PRINT
(makes it $0.39)
** I have (2) $1/4 printables = $3.12 for 8 cans of veggies

Mueller's Pasta—$0.79 ea. or $1.58 BOGO
Use $1/2 from 1/8 SS
(makes it $0.29)
**I have (5) $1/2 newspaper coupons = $2.90 for 10 boxes of pasta

Mt. Olive Sweet Relish or Pickles—$1.20 ea. or $2.40 BOGO
Use $1/1, $0.75/1 from 1/22 SS
(makes it as low as $0.20)
**I have (5) newspaper coupons = $1.00 for 5 jars of pickles

Hall's Cough Drops—$1.00 ea. or $1.46 BOGO
Use $0.50/1 from Feb. *All You* (this will double)
(makes it as low as FREE)
**I have (1) *All You* magazine coupon = $0 for 1 pk. of cough drops
Although this item is not on my target list, I know that at some point
I'm going to need cough drops and I'd rather have them on hand for
free than to have to make a midnight drugstore run and pay full price.

Wish-Bone Dressing—$1.32 ea. or $2.64 BOGO
Use $0.65/2, $0.50/1, $0.70/1 from 1/29 RP
Stack with $1.00/2 Target PRINT
(makes it as low s FREE wyb 2)
Quick note about the salad dressing: to get this product for free we
need the Target printable. Although we have five manufacturer coupons
from the Sunday paper, we can only use one competitor coupon per like
item. With the Target printable the sale would look something like this:
(1) Target printable + (2) $0.50/1 newspaper coupons (will double)
= $0.00 for two bottles of salad dressing. The remaining three would
be $0.32 each. I have (5) newspaper coupons and (1) Target store
coupon = $0.96 for five bottles of salad dressing.

Price Comparison: Retail vs. Pantry Price

Item	Retail Price (per item)	Sensible Stockpiling Price
Veggies	$1.28	8 cans for $3.12
Pasta	$1.58	10 boxes for $2.90
Pickles	$2.40	5 jars for $2.00
Cough drops	$1.46	1 pk. for FREE
Salad dressing	$2.64	5 bottles for $0.96
	5 items total: $9.36	29 items total: $8.98

These sales are from an actual week at one of my favorite local
grocery stores. Look at these items as if you were the one at the store.

Look at the price differences laid out in the chart above. If I were to buy just one of each of these items on a regular shopping day then it would cost me $9.36. However, by shopping when the items are at their rock-bottom price I am able to bring home 29 pantry items for a total of $8.98. Pretty significant savings! Not only that, but look at what this trip has done to our pantry list.

Items to Target

Cheese	Salad dressing	Veggies	Oatmeal
Rice	Crackers	Butter	Mustard
Pickles	Bread	Jelly	Pasta sauce
Chicken	Pasta	Cleaning wipes	Bleach
Shampoo	Detergent	Dryer sheets	Window cleaner
Toothpaste	Toilet paper	Paper towels	Furniture polish

Now pickles, salad dressing, and pasta are marked off for the next twelve weeks and we can focus our attention and our budget on other things.

After you've stocked up for the week, the rest of your grocery budget can go toward those items you still *need*. This cycle continues until you've stocked your pantry with items you use on a regular basis. Then when you run out of pickles, for example, you shop at home. I have a shelf in my garage where I keep some of my pantry items. If I need pickles, I can grab one of my own $0.20 cent jars off the shelf instead of putting it back on my list and paying $2.40.

If you don't make it to the store each week, don't stress about it. The great thing about prices cycling the way they do is that those same sales will come around again.

The Big Picture

As you change your shopping habits and put these ideas into play, your list will start to change. We've talked about that, but now I would like to take just a few minutes to look at how that will happen. It's really kind of fun to see your grocery list shrink week after week until it dwindles down to only a handful of items. Then when you miss a week of shopping, you don't even feel it! (See chart on page 99.)

Month One and Two

At this point your focus has been on changing your shopping habits. It's still early in the game, but you've started building your pantry and you can see where your shelves are fuller than before. Not only that, but there are several items your family uses that you've been able to stock up on. As a result, your list of must-haves is starting to get smaller. It also means that you can now allocate more of your weekly budget toward building your pantry. Instead of $5 to $10, now you've freed up $15 to $20 without increasing what you spend.

Month Three

This is where you really start to notice the difference. By the end of the third month you have been through a twelve-week sale cycle. You know what it feels like to shop from your own pantry, and you often find yourself walking past items you would normally buy, because you know the price will come down soon. Your weekly list is shrinking considerably, to the point where the number of must-haves and the number of pantry items are almost equal.

Month Six

This is what I like to call "maintenance," and it's a beautiful place to be. After six months you have been through two sale cycles and your pantry is stocked. Need shampoo? Just grab some off the shelf. Want spaghetti for dinner? You're covered! You have what you need on hand at any given time, and now you pretty much only shop for those items you have to replenish regularly. Your weekly list is shrinking considerably, to the point where the number of must-haves and the number of pantry items are almost equal.

And Beyond!

The must-have portion of your list has dwindled down to almost nothing and your weekly bill is considerably lower than ever before. This is the goal line! It takes some work to get here, but the reward is oh so wonderful.

Storage Tips

Now that you have all these groceries/household items, you need a place to put them. Yes, we've talked about cleaning out closets and drawers, but let's get a little more specific because I know that some of you are still convinced your baby is going to end up sleeping on a bed made out of toilet paper.

The trick is to look at the space you have in a new way. You'll be amazed at where you can find places to store stuff that you didn't even think about before.

Here are a couple ideas:

- Take some time to go through and clean out bathroom cabinets, linen closets, coat closets, pantries, and any other forgotten space. Get rid of what you don't need, donate what you can, and trash the rest.

- Under the bathroom sink. This long-forgotten area can serve as a great spot for those nonperishable household items you find for pennies on the dollar. Look for cheap stacking baskets or bins at the dollar store to hold items that don't stand up well. Then you can keep everything organized, out of the way, and within reach when you need it. It's always good to store your items where you will end up using them. Out of sight out of mind and all that.

- A second option is to look for a laundry organizer. A good friend of mine has this narrow rolling shelf that slides between her washer and dryer. She uses it to store her supply of laundry detergent, fabric softener, and other cleaning products. It has tons of space, and when it's pushed back you can't even tell it's there. I'm not saying you have to run out and buy this exact organizer, just look at the space you have and think about how you can make the most of it.

- Another fun idea I've seen lately are single shelves placed *over* bathroom doors. It's a great place to add a little extra storage, be it for towels or for your stockpile. And unless you know where to look, you won't even notice it's there.

- Got an empty wall in your laundry room? How about some shelves? Your laundry room is one of those areas that is generally off-limits to guests. And the people who do see it usually love you and won't care if you are using your space to extend your pantry.

- If your cabinets don't go all the way to the ceiling, look at using the top for storage. Just choose your items carefully—you don't want to look like a crazy woman with food hanging out on every flat surface.

- One of my favorite storage methods is this great set of plastic shelves I have out in my garage. They are heavy-duty with plenty of space, meaning I can pack those babies full! In fact, they are often my own personal grocery store when I run out of this or that in the kitchen and need more.

- As your grocery bills shrink, consider saving for a stand-alone freezer. Many times you can find these used but still in great condition. Having a freezer opens a whole new world of possibilities when it comes to building your pantry and keeping food fresh. At this point I don't know how I ever got along without one!

I give you these options to get you thinking. Look around your home as you read this and see all that wasted space you can put to good use. There is no reason to sacrifice the comfort of your family because you bought two hundred tubes of toothpaste and now you have no idea where to put them. (Just kidding, but you get the picture.)

> What if a person has enough money to live on and sees his brother in need of food and clothing? If he does not help him, how can the love of God be in him? My children, let us not love with words or in talk only. Let us love by what we do and in truth. This is how we know we are Christians. It will give our heart comfort for sure when we stand before Him. (1 John 3:17–19 NLV)

Avoiding the Burnout

Burnout. We've all been there. Maybe not with couponing just yet, but you know exactly what I'm talking about. I'm not going to lie; it's easy to burn yourself out couponing. It is so tempting to fall into the trap of feeling like you have to get every deal out there and then beating yourself up when you happen to miss one.

Honey, it is all about balance! I don't want you to burn out. I want you to find that place where this works for you and makes a difference for your family. You'll never get there if you always feel like you're fighting your way upstream in an effort to get all the best deals and lowest prices. Making daily life difficult is not my goal. My goal is to help you build a pantry that works for you. And I don't *think* you can do it—I *know* you can.

Here are a few habits that should be avoided to prevent burnout.

Savings Percentage

I know some couponers who always strive to reach a certain percentage of savings. If they happen to miss that mark one week, then they feel as if they have failed or done something wrong. Don't let yourself fall into this trap. Whether you save 5 percent or 75 percent, you have still saved money.

Marathon Shopping

Let me just be honest with you. There is no way for you to hit every store and snag every deal every week. It's not going to happen. It will consume your life if you let it. I can tell you now that almost every couponer out there struggles with this at some point or another. It is just so easy to get caught up in the mindset that you are missing out on something. Here's the thing: none of us needs this kind of anxiety in our lives. We just don't! And if you feel anxious about missing a sale, it's probably not a good thing.

So prioritize. Make a list of the stores you would like to hit and prioritize them. If you don't get through them all, don't worry about it. Move on to the next week and put the past behind you. See, that's the great thing about couponing. It's not a "one time only" deal where you have to get in line or miss out forever. These deals will come around again. All of them. Yes, I said all of them! Couponing does not have to be overwhelming or stressful. It's about savings and it's about simplicity.

Keeping Up with the Joneses

I talk to new couponers all the time who worry because their stockpile doesn't look like their neighbor's, their friend's, or their sister's. Guess what? It doesn't matter. Honestly, I would be a little worried if your pantry did look exactly like someone else's. Your pantry should be built for your family. Celebrating each other's savings and accomplishments is much more fun than comparing any day.

So far we've talked about how it can benefit you to build a stockpile by saving you trips to the store and buying the things you use at their lowest price. But there are other benefits you might not have considered. Let me tell you a story about my friend Jamie.

The first time we met was entirely by chance—she walked into the first couponing class I ever taught. She was in her midtwenties with four kids under seven, and though her husband worked full-time, it never quite covered everything. They found themselves leaning on food stamps at the beginning of the month and credit cards toward the end of the month just to stay afloat. Jamie wanted more than anything to keep her family from sinking into debt, and she had taken on part-time jobs at Laundromats and fast-food restaurants over the years to help. She later explained to me what drove her to learn how to coupon:

> It was one of the simplest decisions I'd ever made—take on a part-time job or make couponing my part-time job. I was more than willing to work hard at this couponing thing in order to stay home with my family. Within a couple of months we were off of food stamps and I'd built a stockpile that I was really proud of. We still had those tight weeks, sure. But during those weeks I made simple dinners like pasta, tacos, or soup and sandwiches—using ingredients foraged from my stockpile. It made me feel more safe and secure—I could tell things were changing for us. I had absolutely made a big difference for my family just by couponing.

While I love that learning to coupon empowered Jamie to change her family's finances, there's something else about her story that I want to share with you. Just as things were becoming easier for her, one of her friends (we'll call her Melissa) suddenly found herself newly single, in the last semester of nursing school, and devastated—with three kids to care for. What she needed was someone to rescue her in a big way. She honestly needed so many things. Jamie wanted to help any way she could. First of all, there was no way on earth Melissa had time to sit down and learn how to coupon right then. So instead of showing her how to shop, Jamie invited the single mother over to her house to shop in her stockpile.

There was always enough to go around—just like the Bible story with the loaves and fishes. And knowing the kinds of things Melissa's family ate often (easy, convenient meals during this period), Jamie purposefully shopped to stockpile extra of those items. Each week she sent her friend home with a trunk full of groceries and household supplies, even buying sale-priced meat or cheese in bulk so she could send hamburger with the Hamburger Helper or cheese with the taco ingredients.

The amazing part is, this wasn't even giving till it hurt. This was giving painlessly. An extra $10 a week to maintain her stockpile was nearly all the investment Jamie had to make to keep on providing for Melissa until she was in a better place to provide for herself.

Wouldn't we all love to be able to do that? Don't we all have a friend or family member or neighbor who we know is going through a rough patch? Wouldn't it be awesome to have the means to drop off a box of supplies on their doorstep or invite them over to fill a couple bags during a hard week?

Having a stockpile can make a difference not only in your family but also in the lives of those around you who are hurting. I encourage you to keep those people in mind as you look through the lists of free and cheap items each week.

> For God is the one who provides seed for the farmer and then bread to eat. In the same way, he will provide and increase your resources and then produce a great harvest of generosity in you. Yes, you will be enriched in every way so that you can always be generous. And when we take your gifts to those who need them, they will thank God. (2 Cor. 9:10–11)

ACTION STEP

Try your hand at stockpiling.

First, find a nook or cranny in your home that you can use to store some extra items. Maybe it's in your basement or garage, or maybe a shelf in one of your closets can be hijacked for this mission. Once you've claimed a piece of your home for your stockpile, find something to put there!

Head over to Time2SaveWorkshops.com and browse through the ads for grocery or drugstores near you, or look at your favorite store's weekly circular. Usually the best savings are right there on the front or back. Look for an item that your family uses that is at a *really* low price after the sale and coupons are taken into account. You might find only one or two items that you have the right coupons for already, but hey—that's how it is for everyone at the beginning.

Okay, did you spot one item that is super-cheap after the sale price and coupons? Great! That's going to be the item you stock up on this week. Dig out the exact coupons you need, double check to see if there are any extra coupons you can print from home, and see if there are any competitor coupons that you can stack on top—gather those as well.

Put all your coupons in an envelope along with your list. Making a plan and having the coupons all clipped and handy will make your trip much less stressful. Get as many of the item as you can with the coupons you have (even if that's just two or three this first time).

When you get home, tuck your purchases into your little stockpile corner. Step back and pat yourself on the back. You've just started a sensible stockpile!

8

Drugstores and More

What You Don't Know but Should

For we are God's masterpiece. He has created us anew in Christ Jesus, so we can do the good things he planned for us long ago.

Ephesians 2:10

You know those weeks when you sit down to make your shopping list and realize it's "that week"? The week when you have to buy everything, including all of your household supplies? On those weeks, it's so frustrating to get to the grocery store, fill up your cart with toothpaste, toilet paper, laundry detergent, and other household items, and then realize you've blown through your entire grocery budget—and you don't even have any food in the cart yet! In this chapter, I'm going to show you how to save on more than just groceries. You're going to be able to save big money on toiletries, makeup, cleaning supplies, and even online purchases. These categories make up a big chunk of our expenses, so let's talk about how to save there too.

Interested yet? I thought you might be. I know I am! First let me ask you, did you ever think that you could walk into a drugstore and get free toothpaste, expensive razors for under a dollar, and great deals on toilet paper? Me either! But if you've ever couponed at a drugstore before, then you know they are gold mines. They just work a little differently than what you are used to.

The basic idea is that each drugstore chain has its own in-store "currency" you can earn by taking advantage of certain sales and buying specific products. I'll show you how to use that store currency to walk away with super cheap or even free items.

In this chapter I'm going to walk with you through a few of the national drugstore chains, including CVS, Rite Aid, and Walgreens. While we aren't going to cover every single detail, we are going to look at what each store has to offer. There are amazing deals to be had here on things like toothpaste, toothbrushes, cleaning supplies, baby items, razors, razor cartridges (let me repeat that last one . . . *razor cartridges*!), and so much more.

So What's the Big Difference?

The first thing you have to do is take everything you've learned about couponing in a grocery store and chuck it out the window. Drugstore shopping is completely different from grocery store shopping. Shopping at drugstores could be its own book, but I'm going to cover the basics and give you a strong foundation to work with. In addition, I will show you how to find each store's current coupon policy as well as point you toward several online guides to couponing in drugstores.

To begin, let me ask you this: What in the world do you buy at drugstores in the first place? It's a simple question, but one that many of us will have to stop and think about. To get an idea of things you would want to buy at drugstores, get their recent circular, take a trip up and down the aisles, or go to the Time 2 $ave blog and look for the items your family uses in the weekly drugstore matchups. (Yep, we've got matchups for these too.)

Now you are looking for things like toilet paper, paper towels, makeup, cleaning supplies, toothpaste, toothbrushes, diapers, wipes, body wash, shampoo, conditioner, hair products, and Coke. (I'm a Southern girl, so "Coke" refers to all soda, pop, or soft drinks. Don't laugh; you know exactly what I'm talking about!) As you scan through the lists you'll start to notice that each week features a few different items at rock-bottom prices, just like in the grocery stores. If you're at Time 2 $ave, you can click the handy checkboxes next to any items you want to buy, create a list, and print it out. (You'll see your list pop up in the bottom right-hand corner of your screen.)

So far so good? Now, whether you are on the website, in the store, or looking at a circular, you will notice that many of the items listed will earn some kind of store currency. This is the amount you will get back at the register after you purchase certain products. Now you can take that store "money" and buy something else you need.

Have you ever heard of Kohl's Cash or Gym Bucks from Gymboree? This is very similar. It is money given to you by a store to spend in the same store. The requirements are a little different, but the idea is the same.

But let's not get ahead of ourselves here. I want to take this step-by-step 'cause things can get muddy quick.

Step 1: Concentrate on One Drugstore at a Time

First, pick one store. I know, they all have good deals and they all follow similar guidelines, but you will drive yourself two steps from crazy if you try to keep up with everything out there. See, even though they all have similar policies, the differences are in the details. Every store, meaning CVS, Rite Aid, and Walgreens, has its own form of currency and in-store promotions. So take your time, get into the swing of things at your favorite store, and enjoy your savings.

Me? Well, I'm a type A personality and I love a good challenge. By nature I want to tackle all three stores at the same time, and believe me, I have tried. It's not fun. But I have been on a journey to let go of the areas in my life that are stressful. I want to feel at peace and look forward to walking into a store rather than always running from one place to another so fast that I never stop to take a breath. If you take anything from this chapter I hope you will save your sanity and learn from my mistakes. Remember:

There is no pressure.

Don't stress about the stores you don't visit.

Give yourself a pat on the back for choosing balance.

Have fun and enjoy playing the drugstore game.

Step 2: Learning about Your Store

Once you pick your store, it's time to learn all about how that store works. The best way to do this is to go online to their corporate website and read about it. Need a website? Try CVS.com, Walgreens.com, and RiteAid.com. If you see a term you don't understand, try checking appendix C at the back of this book.

While you are at the store's website, look for words such as *specials*, *coupons*, *promotions*, *savings*, and *rewards*. If you see one of these words or others like them, give it a click and see what it has to say. Then register with the site to receive advance notice of sales and other promotional opportunities. Next you want to "like" the store on Facebook, follow them on Twitter, and download store-specific apps if you have a smartphone. This will give you access to coupons and other promotions not found anywhere else. The last step is to sign up for mobile alerts if your cell plan will allow. These messages offer exclusive savings codes you can use in the store.

Step 3: Familiarize Yourself with the Weekly Ad

Drugstore sales run from Sunday to Saturday, and you'll find their weekly ads online and in your Sunday paper.

When looking through the sale ads, pay special attention to the wording around different promotions. Does the ad mention a store loyalty card? Are there any items advertised as free? What about that in-store currency we were talking about?

Since drugstores follow a sale cycle just like grocery stores, each week a small handful of items will be at their lowest price. You'll have to hunt for them as they tend to be sprinkled throughout the ad, but this is where the big savings will be. Our list of matchups on the Time 2 $ave blog will focus on those particular deals.

Step 4: Compare the Ad to the Blog Matchup

If you are using our matchup system at Time 2 $ave, you'll start to notice wording like "Pay $5.99 ~ Get back $3.00" or "It's like paying $2.00!" Let's look at how a drugstore deal might appear on our matchup list.

Contact solution $5.99 ~ Get back $3.99
Use $2/1 PRINT
Pay $3.99 ~ Get back $3.99 (makes it FREE!)

Make sense? Probably not! So let's walk through what this would look like at the drugstore. First you would take the contact solution up to the counter and hand over your store loyalty card if applicable. The item rings up for $5.99. Now hand the cashier your coupon for $2.00 off one bottle of contact solution. This would bring the price down to $3.99 out of pocket (OOP). At this point you would pay the cashier $3.99 plus tax and the register will begin to print your receipt.

But we're not done just yet! Remember the part in the ad where it said "Get back $3.99"? At the bottom of your receipt, or on a separate piece of paper printed after the receipt, you'll see the store currency you've earned on this transaction. In this case you earned $3.99.

Your store currency will be printed with a barcode, which the cashier will scan when you're ready to use it. In other words, the money you get back can only be used in the chain of stores you got it from. So you can't take Extra Care Bucks from CVS and spend them at Walgreens. They have to be used at CVS. But you *can* use that "money" to purchase items in the store or even to pay for your next transaction. (Some exclusions apply, such as milk, prescriptions, beer, and cigarettes.)

Step 5: Multiple Transactions

All right, here's where the rubber hits the road. If you really want to take full advantage of all that drugstores have to offer, then you will need to master the art of multiple transactions. This means that you will take the items in your cart and group them into different transactions based on purchase price and the amount of store currency you will get back. The idea is to minimize your out of pocket expense by "paying" for each transaction with store currency. And let me just say, the clerks and cashiers at the drugstores understand this technique and are used to it. As long as you are considerate and respectful of your fellow customers you shouldn't have any problems.

It's all about the strategy. Remember, our goal is to put the money that we earn from one transaction toward the next one. We are going to strategically plan how to first earn and then spend the store cash before we ever walk in the door. (And a big thanks to my local CVS cashier for being so kind as to teach me how to do this in the first place.) If you are wondering which item to purchase first, choose the one that will cost you the least amount of money out of pocket.

Examples of Multiple Transactions:

Item 1:

> Schick Razors $9.99 ~ Get back $5.99
>
> Pay $9.99
>
> Get back $5.99 (makes it $4.00)

Item 2:

> Colgate Toothpaste $2.00 ~ Get back $1
>
> Use $1/1 coupon
>
> Pay $1 ~ Get back $1.00 (makes it FREE)

Looking at these two examples, the second item would cost you less money out of pocket.

> Item 1—You pay $9.99 OOP and earn $5.99 in store money
>
> Item 2—You pay $1.00 OOP and earn $1.00 in store money

Based on these totals you would purchase item 2 first because you are only spending $1.00 out of your own pocket. Then you would get back $1.00 in store currency that you can put toward your next transaction, the Schick Razors. This will help you lower the OOP amount for that transaction and maximize your savings.

Let's look at another example. This time we will break the items up by transaction.

Item 1:

> Buy (3) Luden's Cough Drops for $5.00 ~ Get back $3.00
>
> Use $1/1 Luden's from 11/13 SS (*Use 3 of these coupons to buy 3 Luden's)
>
> Or use $1/2 from 1/22 SS
>
> Pay as little as $2.00 after coupons ~ Get back $3.00 (makes it FREE + $1 overage if you have the $1/1 coupons)

Item 2:

> Spend $10 on Nivea Lip Care, priced at $2.50 each ~ Get back $3.00
>
> Use $3/2 from 2/12 SS (*Use 2 of these coupons to buy 4 Nivea products)
>
> Pay $4 after coupons ~ Get back $3.00 (makes it $1 for all 4 items)

Item 3:

> Tylenol Precise $7.49 ~ Get back $2.00
>
> Use $5/1 from 2/19 RP
>
> Pay $2.49 after coupons ~ Get back $2.00 (makes it $0.49)

For this example we have three items we want to buy and we are going to group them into three transactions so that we can use the store money earned from one to help pay for the others.

Transaction #1

> Buy (1) Tylenol Precise = $7.49
>
> Use (1) $5/1 coupon from the 2/19 RP
>
> Pay $2.49 ~ Get back $2.00

Transaction #2

> Buy (3) Luden's Cough Drops = $5.00
>
> Use (3) $1/1 Coupons from the 11/13 SS
>
> Use $2 store currency (earned from the Tylenol transaction)
>
> Pay $0.00 ~ Get back $3.00

Transaction #3

> Buy (4) Nivea Lip Care items = $10.00
>
> Use (2) $3/2 coupons from the 2/12 SS
>
> Use $3.00 store currency (earned from the Luden's transaction)
>
> Pay $1.00 OOP ~ Get back $3.00

The total amount you paid out of pocket after all three transactions was just $3.49 plus tax. You are now left with $3 in store currency. That's like getting all these products for $0.49! The great part about this process is once you start you often leave with store currency in hand, meaning that your OOP for next week's transactions will be even less because that currency can be carried over and used at a later date.

Step 6: Plan of Attack

The key to this whole system is having a plan of attack in place before you step foot in the store. I've learned that my trips to drugstores run much smoother if I know what I want to buy and take the time to plan out my transactions in advance. That's not to say my plans don't change once I get there. After all, you never know when an item will be out of stock. But at least I know what I'm looking for.

Now let me tell you, some days in drugstores are easier than others. There will be times when plans get derailed and things don't work out the way you want them to. Maybe you walk in with a perfect list, only to head straight for your first item and find that it's out of stock. Just like your second item and maybe even your third. But don't let it get you down. Honey, it's just not worth it. These are coupons; it is so not worth getting stressed out about.

These days I know when I walk in that plans could change, and I'm okay with that. When it happens you might just find me parked in the middle of the candy aisle as I recalculate with a pen and paper. I'm not saying this is the perfect solution for everyone, but that's how I roll. And I do have a few tips to help things run a bit smoother.

To make my trip easier I always print out my list and put the coupons I will be using for the trip in an envelope. If I know I am going to do multiple transactions this week, then I will take the extra step of giving each transaction its own envelope.

Remember me telling you that I'm unorganized, have ADHD, and hate math? This is why I make a point to separate my transactions. It helps me to not get distracted as I'm working my way around the store. If I don't do this, I always end up buying the wrong things together and messing up my savings.

So here is my system. When I walk into the store and get a cart, I also grab three shopping baskets. I prefer not to do more than three transactions, because that is how long my attention span lasts. I separate each transaction into its own basket with the corresponding coupon envelope. Two baskets fit horizontally on the back of the cart and the third goes underneath.

Once I finish my first transaction, basket number 2 stacks inside basket number 1 and I am ready to go. I also go ahead and put any store currency I just earned into the second envelope with the coupons I am about to use. Finish up with transaction number 2 and then repeat the whole process a third time.

This is just my own system. It may or may not work for you, and that's fine. You have to find whatever works for you and go with it.

Step 7: How Often Should I Shop at Drugstores?

I used to try to go every single week. That didn't last long. Talk about burnout! Now I just go once or twice a month, depending on our schedule. The thing to remember is to keep it all in perspective. Whether you save 5 percent, 20 percent, or 70 percent, you are still saving money. So ignore the little voices in your head telling you about all the things you missed out on and enjoy the savings you scored.

And More!

Remember when I said that this chapter was about much more than just drugstores? Did you know you can earn rewards just by doing the things you have always done? Like shopping! There are several great online sites that give you the chance to earn cash back on everything you buy, but my personal favorite is ebates.com. Ebates is pretty straightforward, and I have to say I love the way it works. All you do is sign up for an account, browse through the more than fifteen hundred stores they partner with, click on the store's link . . . and shop! Once you click your favorite store, a tracking ticket is created to track your purchases to ensure proper credit. You are then directed to your favorite store to shop as you normally would. By going through Ebates for your online purchases you can earn a certain percentage of cash back from each store. That percentage will vary based on the store you are shopping at and their current promotion, but either way the money is automatically credited to your Ebates account. Once every three months or so you will receive a check from Ebates for the cash back you've earned. It's that simple.

Hidden Savings

Are you in the military? Are you a teacher? Maybe you're a senior or a student. If so, then there are additional savings floating around out there that you may be missing. Many businesses, including stores, restaurants, and attractions, offer special pricing for military, teachers, seniors, and students. To find out if they do, just ask. You might score extra savings just by being who you are!

Keep in mind that many places require you to show a military, teacher, or student ID to get these special savings. So keep your ID handy and get ready to save some cash.

Freebies

Sometimes companies will offer totally free items to entice us to try them out. This is a really fun perk to look out for when you're hunting down deals.

For example, a photo company might offer a promo code for a free photo book because they hope you'll fall in love with their product and begin using them on a regular basis. In addition, freebies are often available when new products hit the market. For instance, I recently received a free full-size Downy product just for filling out a questionnaire.

Free sample offers come down the pike all the time as well. If you have a moment to sign up for these along the way, you could be opening your mailbox a couple times a week to purse-size fragrance samples or travel-size Aveeno lotions or packets of Wisk laundry detergent.

Other Great Deals

What if you could save money shopping for clothes, office supplies, home improvement projects, baby items, and more? Most of us are creatures of habit and have become so used to paying a certain amount for the above items that we don't necessarily think there is an alternative. Once you know where to look and what kind of savings or promotions to expect, it will become second nature.

Eating Out

Just because we are saving money on our groceries doesn't mean we can't enjoy eating out, especially when there are so many great offers available. Many restaurants offer coupons, freebies, or savings clubs if you sign up for updates online. Wait, don't toss that receipt away without taking a quick peek. Many restaurants offer freebies or a percentage off if you call the number at the bottom of your receipt and answer a couple of survey questions. Recently I signed up to receive text messages from my family's favorite restaurant. I usually get one or two texts per week alerting me about new deals.

One more thing: just like some grocery stores accept competitor coupons, some restaurants will do the same. I noticed just this week that one of my favorite sub shops accepts coupons from any competitor.

Want free food on your birthday? We've got a list of birthday freebies on the Time 2 $ave blog. If you can't find what you are looking for, take a moment and either Google the restaurant or give them a call. Obviously you can't eat at ten different places on your birthday, so don't feel like you've got to sign up for every birthday freebie known to man. Birthday freebies and offers usually expire quickly. When I first started couponing I signed up for more birthday freebies and offers than I could use in a year. Save yourself some time, pick out your favorites, and don't worry about the rest.

Shopping Malls and Retail Stores

Each week on the Time 2 $ave blog we post sales and coupons from our favorite mall and retail stores. If you go online and sign up for updates, you'll get all kinds of offers sent to you. From coupons and freebies through the mail to emails and text messages like I mentioned above, you won't have to look for savings.

Remember how you can earn back a percentage of your total sale in the form of cash? Here's a little secret: all of these savings I've included are in addition to earning cash back on your total purchase. Are you wondering if it's worth it? Let me break down an example for you:

Favorite retail store coupon:	$25 off every $50 purchase + free shipping
Cash back reward:	6%
Total purchase amount:	$100.00 **check out in two transactions
First transaction total:	$50.00 - ($25 off every $50 purchase coupon code) = $25.00 (save 50%)
Second transaction:	$50.00 - ($25 off every $50 purchase coupon code) = $25.00 (save 50%)
Total coupon savings:	**$50.00**
Cash back reward:	**6% of total purchase**
Transaction 1: Transaction 2:	$25 x 6% = $1.50 $25 x 6% = $1.50
Total cash back:	$3.00
Coupon savings:	$50 + cash back $3 **= $53.00 total saved**

Note: to maximize my savings I will need to check out in two transactions. Otherwise I would only receive $25 off of my total purchase of $100. If I separate my transactions, I'll save $25 off of $50 each time I check out.

You will find that retail stores that you frequent *want* you to sign up for their special offers so you'll keep coming back. For example, I'll never forget the day I found out that my favorite local toy store offers a loyalty card. Each time I shop, they stamp my purchase amount. Then after ten trips I get a voucher worth 10 percent of my total purchases. Loyalty programs offer fantastic deals and require very little effort, but the savings can be substantial.

Office Supplies

I can't count how many times I've been asked if the price of ink and paper to print coupons outweighs the savings benefits. Let's get that myth out of the way; of course you can still save tons of money. Besides, if you shop at any of the big office supply stores you'll quickly discover that there are amazing deals to be had through their rebate programs. You can find information about each store's rebate program either online or in the store. It's a great way to score cheap, if not free, office supplies throughout the year. I'm not just talking pencils, either. Paper, ink, school supplies, you name it.

There are ways to save money on just about everything you buy. The first step is keeping your eyes open for discounts. Once you know they are there, you'll know what to look for. Keep your eyes open, ask questions when necessary, and enjoy!

Making Sense of the Madness

Are all these deals starting to pile up on you? No worries. That's what I'm here for. If you want to know the latest and greatest of what sales are floating around in cyberspace, then just stop by the Time 2 $ave blog at www.time2saveworkshops.com. The truth is I would love to list every deal out there right here in this book for you to read about, but they are always changing! That's why I send you to the blog. It's the place you can get up-to-the-minute deals on the items you love.

So check back and check back often. We update the site with deals and coupons roughly ten to twenty times a day so that you don't miss out on anything.

Now, what will you do with all these great deals and freebies you're about to get? One of the things I have done is to start a gift closet. That way I can take advantage of all the freebies I come across and then use them later for birthday, shower, or even Christmas presents.

Examples? Well, how about free pictures or photo books, free stationery, free T-shirts, free baby products, or super cheap toys. And that's just what I've seen this week.

You can also take some of the free or cheap toiletries and household items you've scored at the drugstore, pack them into a laundry basket, and give them as a housewarming present or a college dorm survival kit.

The basis of this whole chapter is that I want to open your eyes to the world of savings that exists beyond the grocery store. Yes, we coupon. And yes, we can use that to save a huge amount of money on our groceries. But that is only the beginning. Once you get into the mindset of saving money you can find deals on just about anything you want to buy. All you have to do is look.

ACTION STEP

Let's get something for free at a drugstore this week!

Start by picking just one drugstore to focus on for this first trip. Go to that store's website and learn what their store currency is called (for instance, CVS calls theirs Extra Care Bucks, or ECBs in coupon lingo). Get familiar with their coupon policy as well. Now head over to Time2SaveWorkshops.com and locate that store's current weekly ad, or pick up a copy from the store (you'll also find links to tutorials about each drugstore at the top of each week's matchups). Look for an item that allows you to earn store currency, especially one that will be free after this reward is taken into account. There is usually at least one item per week, per drugstore, that will give you back the same amount of store currency you paid out of pocket. If there is a coupon involved, that brings your OOP expense down further—even better! I would suggest picking one or two backup items to try as well, just in case your first choice is out of stock when you arrive.

Now head to the drugstore (with any necessary coupons in hand) and buy that item. Make sure to get the exact size or variety described in the ad, and don't forget to hand over your store loyalty card before you check out. (You can usually sign up for those in the store and use them right away.) Once you have paid and receive your store reward, you are finished. You can either save that reward to experiment with next week or buy another item that you need from this week's sale ad.

9

Peelie Stealers Go Home!

You may have noticed that people tend to have preconceived ideas about couponers. Unfortunately, somewhere along the way couponers have gotten a bad rap. Well, we're out to change all that. Being a considerate and ethical couponer can make a world of difference for you and for those around you.

Develop Relationships with Your Cashiers and Store Employees

There are times when store employees we come in contact with have the ability to make our lives easier or harder. They can help us find the things we are looking for, or they can shrug their shoulders as they turn and walk the other way. How do you want them to respond to you?

I know what I want: I want to be the customer who makes the effort to know their names. I want to ask them how they're doing and take an interest in their lives, not just ask if they can find me another box of Cheerios. Do I do this to try to get the inside track on all the best sales? Not in the least. I do it because these are people I interact with on a regular basis and it's a simple and kind thing to do.

I enjoy hearing stories of people who have favorite cashiers they love to see—people they've come to know and look for when they walk in the store. With minimal effort we can bring a smile to their faces and make their day just a little bit better. They get to deal with the worst. We've all seen it, we all know it happens, and it's not who *we* want to be.

Be Kind and Encouraging to Other Shoppers

Do to others as you would like them to do to you. (Luke 6:31)

We are all in the same boat here. You and I aren't the only people out there struggling to save money; it's a tough time for lots of folks. That's why I encourage you to be as kind and helpful as you can to other shoppers. If someone walks up to you in the store and asks a question about your coupons or what you are doing, try to help them out by sharing some of your knowledge. If they follow you out to your car with that curious look but seem too afraid to actually talk to you, go ahead and strike up a conversation. When you find yourself in the checkout line next to a lady with a cart full of items that you have extra coupons for, offer her a few of your coupons. It's also fun to just leave extra coupons on the shelf for others to find and use. I love being a "coupon fairy"!

The thing about being positive and encouraging is that you will always be glad you were. Never once have I regretted being kind to someone. Never. Besides, I fully believe that we reap what we sow. I like to put it this way: you're not going to plant oranges and end up with bananas. So be the person you would like to see in others. You might just be amazed at the rewards that come your way.

Keep Calm and Carry On

The reality is that couponing trips don't always go as planned. They just don't. I remember one trip to Kmart where I had all these coupons lined up based on a promotion they were running. I had already made a trip on Thursday, and I came back on Friday to go through again.

Well, guess what? When I got up to the register the cashier looked at me sheepishly and said that they were no longer honoring that promotion. "Since when?" I asked, knowing I had gotten this exact same sale just the day before. "Since this morning," she replied. The poor girl braced, like she was waiting for me to jump down her throat. I didn't. I wasn't even planning on it. Instead I smiled, thanked her for letting me know about the change, and then said that I would just go ahead and put my items back.

She looked absolutely shocked. She stammered repeatedly that I didn't have to do that and kept asking me if I was mad. I assured her I wasn't, smiled again, and then went on about my day.

By her reaction I can tell you this is not how other customers had responded to that news. But guess what? That sweet little cashier standing across from me doesn't make the policy; she's simply told to enforce it. And in most cases she can get in some pretty big trouble for bending it. So what good is it going to do me to yell at her?

Here's the truth of the matter: it's just a coupon. It's not the end of the world, and it's not really going to change your life one way or the other if you can't get this or that deal.

Have Realistic Expectations

I want you to finish this book with realistic expectations. You aren't going to go out there and pay $4.00 a week for your groceries and I'll never tell you to strive for that goal. I want you to know what true savings look like on a weekly basis.

What do expectations have to do with being considerate or ethical? Here's an example that most everyone can relate to: being in a hurry. I've got issues with being on time. Church starts every Sunday at the same time, 10:00 a.m. Our church is about twenty miles away from our house. I can't expect to leave my house at 9:55 and still arrive at church at 10:00. It's just not going to happen. It's going to take some extreme behavior, like breaking the speed limit, running stop signs, and defying gravity to achieve that unrealistic goal.

The same applies to couponing. We're all revved up and raring to go, but it's impossible to leave the grocery store every week with $300 of groceries for free or even for $2. If that's my goal, I'm going to end up bending some rules to get there. At the very least, I'm setting myself up for serious frustration.

Trust me, I've been there. Once you start saving money it's easy to want to up your game and save more. It can become a kind of competition you have with yourself to do better and better each week. It took me some time to realize that focusing on a certain percentage of savings instead of doing the best I could for this season of my life was not going to end well. Don't focus on the savings or the deals that you don't get. Instead, I encourage you to think about the ones that you do. Look at the money you have saved and the difference it has made in your family's life. That is what success looks like!

Peeling the Peelies

I'm not going to lie; you will be tempted to bend the rules. At some point, you'll find a display of your favorite cereal with a bright shiny peelie on every box. (Yay!) But it's not on sale here. (Boo!) Wouldn't you know, this cereal is on sale at another grocery store across town and these exact peelies would make the cereal free over there. If only you peeled off, say, five, ten, or . . . umm . . . twenty and ran across town with them—you could be rolling in free cereal for the rest of your days!

I'll be totally honest with you, there was a time as a new couponer when I peeled those coupons off the boxes and stuffed them in my binder without a second thought. But when you get away with it once, it's that much harder to say no the next time. I had to make a personal decision about this years ago; it's just not something I feel comfortable doing. I ran into my store manager one night. He was kneeling on the floor, looking through boxes of crackers on a display. They all had a shiny square where a peelie had once been but now was mysteriously missing. He was confused as to why any of his customers would take the coupon and not buy the crackers, since he'd set them all out so they wouldn't miss the deal. I knew that I wouldn't take one while he watched, and that told me I would no longer take one when he wasn't looking either.

I later learned that brands occasionally track where a peelie is redeemed, so it has a negative impact on the store that lost its supply of peelies to the competitor down the road. Beyond that, I've seen

Ways to Save Money When You Need a Break from Couponing

Yes, we all fight it. If you haven't already experienced it, there will be weeks when you just don't feel like couponing. You might have gotten behind on organizing your coupons, or maybe life has just been too busy. I've got two kids playing ball, which comes out to two games per week. Many of you who are parents can relate. There have been times when I avoided going to the grocery store because I didn't have my stuff together. However, there are ways I can still save money and take the pressure off myself.

- BOGO deals. Most people think it means that if you buy one item you get the other one free. But if an item is advertised at $4.20 BOGO, it doesn't always mean that the first item costs $4.20 and the second one is free. Instead, in some stores, the price is cut in half between the two. Both items are $2.10 each. The great thing is that in this case you don't have to purchase both. Purchasing BOGO items is a great way to save money, even without coupons, because the price is already cut in half.

- Shop at discount stores, and buy generic at national retail stores. Another option is purchasing in bulk at warehouse stores.

Or . . . if you can't bear to shop without coupons, pick five items from your favorite store's list and forget the rest. Take the pressure off of yourself. Too often I've felt that if I'm going to make it to the grocery store I have to get as many sale items as I can. Instead, I have learned that a thirty-minute power trip to help stock my pantry sometimes works best.

how frustrated it can make other shoppers when they see that bright shiny spot where the peelie used to be. So for me, unless I'm buying the product, the peelies stay on the shelf.

Tear Pads Are for Sharing

Tear pads, blinkies, and other random stacks of coupons you'll find at the store are meant to benefit as many people as possible. Everyone would like a chance at those savings, but unfortunately, I've seen my store put out a tear pad at 9:00 in the morning and have it completely gone by 9:30. I know it may be tempting to take the whole stack and run, but that's when you take a deep breath, remain calm, and pat yourself on the back for just taking two. Look how kind you were to the next twenty couponers who showed up.

There will be a day when you are thrilled to find the last lonely slip still clinging to the tear pad. In that moment you will be grateful that someone else didn't come by and strip it clean.

I like to say, "Take two the Time 2 $ave way." This gives you a chance to get a great deal (twice!) and also leaves plenty to go around for anyone else who might like a chance.

Use Store Coupons Correctly

I remember when I first started couponing that store coupons were kind of a gray area for me. I knew that you could only use them at certain stores, but I wasn't quite sure how they fit into the big picture. Now I know that when you use a store coupon those funds come directly out of that store's advertising budget. Simply put, they don't get reimbursed. Plus, when a store chooses to double coupons, they also don't get reimbursed for the part that is doubled. These are ways they get us in the door and keep us happy campers.

Knowing this has made me more aware of store coupons and how I use them. I love being able to stack a store coupon on a manufacturer coupon. I love when stores double my coupons. That's a big part of how we get those great prices. So I don't want to abuse the privilege. Paying attention to the wording and keeping up with current polices is part of playing fair. If it says I only get one deal per coupon, then that's all I get.

Don't Take Coupons Out of Papers You Don't Buy

Ugh . . . I've had this happen more times than I want to remember. On our way home from church on Sunday afternoon, we'd swing by the store to pick up a couple newspapers. Imagine my surprise when I got home and started digging through them only to find that half of my papers have been stripped of their inserts.

Talk about a major letdown! Now I'm signed up with a newspaper delivery service. However, if you are purchasing your paper at the store, always look through it before you leave the store.

Pulling coupons from papers you don't buy is stealing. Plus, many small vendors who sell papers operate on tiny profit margins, all the way down to a few pennies. Snagging the coupons hurts their sales and their income.

Coupon Fraud

We're just about done with all the "dos and don'ts," but there's one big don't left. The *biggest* don't. Addressing coupon fraud is a necessary evil. We really need to cover it, not because I'm worried that any of you will do it but because you need to understand what it is so you can avoid it.

Coupon fraud happens when a person uses a coupon for an item they did not purchase or does not satisfy the terms of redemption. It also refers to a store seeking to redeem a coupon for a product they have not sold.[1]

What does this look like in the real world? One example of coupon fraud is copying a coupon.

When a coupon is printed off the internet it is given its own unique code that is tied to your computer's IP address. This code changes each time the offer is printed. So when a printable is copied, the company

1. "Frequently Asked Questions," Coupon Information Corporation, http://www.couponinformationcenter.com/faq.php.

can tell exactly when and where it was printed in the first place. The bottom line is that copying coupons is considered counterfeiting. These are just coupons!

Other examples of fraud include trying to redeem coupons for products you didn't buy and using expired coupons. The crazy part is that people do this all the time, knowingly slipping extra coupons into a stack at the register or cutting off the expiration dates. Girl, that's crazy! I'll say it again, these are just coupons! And even if an unsuspecting cashier lets it slide once in a while, in the end who should be your moral compass: you or a cashier who doesn't know any better?

Another thing to look out for is plain old counterfeit coupons. In case you never watched *Extreme Couponing*, one episode featured a teenager who had purchased dozens of coupons over the internet for totally free packs of toilet paper. A red flag went up when I watched it, and it went up for the manager too, as he manually deducted hundreds of dollars from the young man's order when the coupon wouldn't scan properly. Fast forward a couple weeks later, and it turns out that the store could not get reimbursed for those hundreds of dollars in fake coupons. They in turn forced the young man and his mother to come up with the money. Doesn't that whole story just leave a bad taste in your mouth? Luckily, if you ever suspect an internet coupon is a fake, you can check it out at the Coupon Information Center's website (http://www.couponinformationcenter.com).

Don't Leave Who You Are in the Car

You may never find yourself in any of the situations above, but I can't promise that you won't be tempted somewhere along the way. A good motto to keep in mind is, "Don't leave who you are in the car." I tell people in my live workshops that coupons are not worth pitching a fit over. They're not worth being selfish or rude. Becoming a crazy coupon lady is not the goal here; it's certainly not what I want to be remembered for. I don't want to be known one way at church or with my friends and family and another way at the grocery store. I want very much to be a light and a testimony everywhere I go and to love those around me no matter what.

From experience I can tell you that many times God has opened the door for me to witness to others at the grocery store. Yes, the grocery store. Right there between the bright boxes of cereal and the giant super packs of toilet paper. The setting may seem strange, but if he opens that door then I want to be obedient enough to walk through it.

This is a case where these words of Jesus come to mind:

> "Love the Lord your God with all your heart and with all your soul and with all your mind and with all your strength." The second is this: "Love your neighbor as yourself." There is no commandment greater than these. (Mark 12:30–31 NIV)

ACTION STEP

Recognize those who help you.

I have a challenge for you. When was the last time you sought out a manager just to tell them how wonderful one of their employees is? Well, the next time you go to the store and someone is helpful to you, make a point to find their boss or another store manager and just share how pleasant they made your shopping experience. It brightens the manager's day because most people only want to talk to them if they have a complaint. It helps your favorite employee and will usually earn them some form of recognition. And it will make you feel pretty darn great for the rest of the day. It's a win-win all the way around!

ACTION STEP

Strike up a conversation with a cashier.

As you work your way through the checkout line, consider asking your cashier how their day is going. And then listen. Make eye contact and smile at them, encouraging them to share their story and to actually *talk* to you. These people have lives outside of work just like we do, and they often have amazing stories to tell. So strike up a conversation. You might just be surprised at what you will hear.

10

Time 2 $ave, Time 2 Give

And I have been a constant example of how you can help those in need by working hard. You should remember the words of the Lord Jesus: "It is more blessed to give than to receive."

Acts 20:35

The vision behind this book reaches beyond finding deals. It's about giving. It's about bringing hope. And it's about making a difference.

This final chapter sends you off into the world to make a difference, not just in your own wallet or bank account, but also in the life of your neighbor, a local shelter, a struggling family member, or your church. I've come to realize that if we don't take purposeful steps to live out what we believe and are called to do, it won't happen. A lifestyle of giving supported by using coupons enables us to live out the passion of influencing our world.

How many of you have wanted to do something for someone else but were never in the financial position to do so? Something as simple as a coupon can be the tool you use to invest in someone in need. Not only can you make a difference in the lives of others, you can also teach valuable lessons to your family and friends. Remember Jamie's story? She used her skills to help a friend in a way she never thought would be possible. Now I'll teach you how to pass on to your children, friends, or loved ones the legacy of:

- Giving to those you come in contact with.
- Appreciating what we do have and are now able to get.
- Being thankful that even in need we are still very blessed.
- Valuing delayed gratification.
- Saving big so you can give bigger.
- Instilling the virtues of empathy, selflessness, and kindness toward others.
- Empowering entire families to work together as a team.

The most interesting thing about this journey is that we all start from the same place. We start from a place of need—financial need to be specific. A place where we know we need help and we are willing to try anything to get it. Like couponing!

Even if you aren't facing a financial crisis, you probably know someone who is or someone who has. If you have managed to come through this time of job loss and uncertainty unscathed, this chapter is still for you. You may have the best job, a fully funded retirement account, cars with that lovely new smell, and a vacation home in Hawaii . . . yet it feels as if something is still missing in your life. And that something is the pleasure of giving a gift. The journey that helped me to find this missing piece nearly broke me, but it's one that I want to share with you.

We've been spending quite a bit of time together over these pages, just chatting over coffee and coupons. I feel like we're friends, and I want to ask you something. When you think of my story, what comes to mind? I'd venture that most of you would say, "You have made it to the other side. You faced financial devastation, learned to coupon, and are now using those skills to help others." I'm telling you, I can almost hear the violins humming in the background to the tune of "It's a Wonderful Couponing World," and it's a pretty nice place to be.

In fact, it's not just about what happened, it's about what is happening even now. As I am finishing up this book, God is calling me back to an all-too-familiar place. My husband is a pharmaceutical rep and his main drug just went generic. We woke this morning anxiously awaiting the call from corporate to find out if his job would be eliminated. The last time we waited on the same kind of phone call, it was the day after my father's funeral a little over three years ago. My heart screams with doubt, *We've already been through this twice in the last eight years. And now again? You have got to be kidding me.*

At the same time, I hear God gently whisper in my spirit, "Remember where I've brought you from. I did not forsake you then and I won't now." I know he is calling me to take his hand and trust his heart. To trust in his promises more than in the security of a job.

The phone call came and went. It wasn't the answer I had hoped for. It wasn't the answer that I wanted. I'm back in the place where I started couponing. I don't know what the future holds, but I know Who holds the future.

But the journey to get to this place was anything but fun.

It's not something I choose to focus on as God has been faithful to redeem my life and lead me into the light of a new day. He walks with me each day, supporting me when I struggle and even carrying me completely in those moments when I still feel as if I might shatter. During those times it is important that I remind myself of just how far God has brought me. I tell you from the bottom of my heart, I have walked through the fire, and I mean it. I'm not being dramatic, not trying to add interest or intrigue to my story; I'm just sharing the truth.

Five years ago I faced a reality that shook me to my core. My family had two spec houses that sat empty for over two years. This meant that each month we faced three mortgages and three sets of bills and upkeep.

Then, my father, one of the true lights of my life, was diagnosed with incurable brain cancer and there was *nothing* I could do to help him. Nothing I could do to stop the pain and nothing that would shield me from watching this once vibrant man become helpless, unable to walk, unable to sit, unable to even turn over in his own bed.

I was blessed to be with my father as he took his last breath and was ushered into the presence of the Lord God Almighty. I held that moment with me as I struggled through the next few days, facing the necessities that go hand in hand with death and marking my days one hour, one minute at a time.

Everywhere I turned I faced nothing but pain, heartbreak, devastation, and despair. It was the darkest season of my life. I felt as if I would never walk in the light again. How could I survive this? Only by the grace of God. If not for that grace, this book would never have been written. And if it were, it wouldn't have been by me, because I wanted to die. I thought I was going to die.

My life was in pieces and what remains is a girl who has been humbled to the very core of her soul. I'm not the same person I was that day. I never will be and I never want to be because what remains has been pieced back together in a way that is beautiful. Not outer beauty; that's subjective, eye of the beholder and all that. I mean the beauty of someone who knows what it feels like to be carried in the arms of God. Not out of want or folly, but out of a desperate and devastating need that *flung* me into my Savior's arms.

If it were up to me I would have walked on my own. I'm the girl who can *handle* life. I hold my head up as I walk through the storm and I face the world on *my* terms. I don't cry. At least, I didn't. Now I think back and wonder, *Was I really that strong?* Of course not. None of us are, no matter how perfectly our armor fits. I was impressed with myself, but the world was definitely not impressed with me. I remember back in college when a good friend told me, "Kasey, your last name is perfect because you wear your armor well!" My maiden name was Knight.

Today, I'm a hot mess. I cry. I stumble. I fail. And I get back up because I realize that I don't *have* to carry myself. I have someone much stronger by my side who is willing to do it for me. Now I know that I don't have to *be* anything for anyone. I don't have to put on a show or dance around like a performing monkey hoping you will like me. I mean, don't get me wrong, I want you to like me! I'd love to hang out over some gummy worms and a Diet Coke. But the difference is I am going to be me. Take it or leave it. What you see is what you get—all six-foot tall, unorganized, ADHD, leg-shaking, ants in her pants crazy girl. Yes, I just said I was crazy, but you know that. We're friends, remember?

Right about now I bet you are wondering what in the heck is going on here. Did someone snag your couponing book and replace the last chapter with something completely different and random? Why does any of this even matter?

It matters because it is where my journey began. I share it because I want you to understand my starting point before we talk about what happened next. More than that, I *need* you to understand that this book, my whole life, is a testament to the grace of God. He took this simple country girl and turned her life upside down, inside out, and around. He moved me from emptiness to abundance, from misery and despair to contentment and expectancy. How? Partially with coupons.

Yep, those itty-bitty slips of nothing that beep at the grocery check-out when you buy toilet paper are the very thing God has used to perform miracles in my life and in the lives of hundreds of others. I am amused and amazed at the same time when I think about how creative God is. Coupons? Seriously, never in a million years would I have guessed that God would reach deep into that particular pit.

Remember my ketchup story? I know I bring it up a lot, but that moment marked a true turning point in my life. I didn't recognize this turning point when I went every day and bought another bottle of ketchup. I was just excited.

And (okay, I'll admit it!) there is that fun little part of me that loves to shop. When you have no money you can't go shopping. Ketchup became my shopping fix. I know, I know . . . it isn't a cute outfit, but at the time it really did make me feel like I was getting to splurge a little. Don't laugh—there will come a day when you find yourself skipping out of the grocery store, receipt in hand as you struggle not to shout to the heavens about how much you just saved.

At some point over the next couple of weeks I remember thinking to myself that if I got ketchup for $0.16, salsa for $0.36, toothpaste for free, and canned veggies for nothing, then why couldn't I start sharing this blessing with others? My income had not changed. We still had three mortgages and my husband was still unemployed, but my pantry had started to overflow and our bank account had stopped leaking money.

From that day forward I started looking at my grocery list a bit differently. Now it wasn't just about my family. Now it was about what I could do to help someone else. Each time I sat down to make out my list I would look at every item with a new purpose. Is this something I could donate? Is it something that would be helpful to someone else? I started buying things just to give them away. Here I was smack in the middle of the most challenging financial situation of my life and

I was able to give more than ever before. And not the old dusty can of rutabagas lurking in the back of my pantry that may or may not be older than my children. (Right about now I can hear about 90 percent of you saying, "What's a rutabaga?" It's a vegetable. My grandmother used to cook it all the time fresh out of her garden. Super yummy, I promise!) It may sound awful, but I can remember standing in front of my pantry trying to decide which canned food I liked the least because that was going to be my donation item. I know—terrible, but true. I'm just being real here.

Today giving has become an integral part of my family's lifestyle. It's exciting and we look forward to it. It's fun to donate! Icing, cake mixes, pickles, party mix, oatmeal, canned veggies, juice, bottled water, toothpaste, candles, shampoo, makeup, body wash—I could keep going on here, but for the sake of my own attention span I think you get the picture. Grocery shopping used to be something I dreaded. What was there to look forward to? I'd walk out of the store irritated by how much money I'd spent for so few items and knowing I'd be back soon to repeat the cycle. Sounds miserable, doesn't it?

Once the veil was lifted I began to see opportunities to give all around me. It was during this time that my focus started to change. Instead of focusing on my own situation, I began thinking about how I could reach out to others. It all started with simple questions. It seemed like every time I walked into the store someone would stop me and ask, "What are you doing?" or "How are you doing this?" They would tell me how they had just lost their job or how they were trying to care for an entire family on a single income.

I remember one night in particular when a lady stopped me. She was shopping with her elderly mother and was extremely curious about what I was doing and how this whole coupon thing worked. We started talking and she shared how her husband had lost his job, her own pay had just been cut in half, and her daughter and son-in-law had been forced to move in with her after they lost their jobs, home, and car. Now she was the primary breadwinner for this large family.

As we walked around the grocery store together, I showed her sale items, shared my coupons, and soaked up her excitement. Then, when we finally made it to the checkout counter, she was able to save over $115 on her groceries that night. It was absolutely precious to see how excited they were to watch their grocery bill drop a bit each time a coupon was scanned. They had purchased more food than they were normally able to and had paid considerably less for it. They were so happy, and yet I was the one who was truly blessed that night. I had been given the privilege of helping this family and it was so wonderfully humbling.

That night was not a coincidence. It was what I like to call a "God-incidence." I am a firm believer that I will reap what I sow. I'm not going to plant bananas and then grow oranges. The law of the harvest never changes. I believe that if I plant kindness, goodness, empathy, and generosity, I will reap the same in my own life.

I didn't do anything special that night except share what had brought hope to my family's finances, but it shows why I am so passionate about couponing. I know what it's like to feel defeated. I also know what it feels like to hope. And that is what coupons are to me. They're hope. They have the power to open doors of opportunity in ways you never thought possible.

What Does Giving Look Like?

Giving can be anything you want it to be for your family because there is no right or wrong way to give. The reality is that no matter how you choose to give it is an act that has the power to bless you in amazing ways. I've heard testimonies of families who feel closer and marriages that have grown stronger. Today you have the power to create a new legacy for your family. One of new traditions, new opportunities to spend time together as a family, and a new focus on helping others.

To get you started, here are a couple examples of places that always need help.

What goes where?

Grocery, personal care items, and household items: food banks, homeless shelters, battered women's shelters, local church food pantry, Salvation Army, United Way

Pet food: animal shelters, churches

School supplies: schools, day cares, Salvation Army, churches

Baby items: teen pregnancy centers, food banks, homeless shelters, battered women's shelters, churches, Salvation Army, United Way

Who can you help?

Homeless people: make baggies of personal care items such as toothbrush, toothpaste, nonperishable food like snack crackers, lip balm, shampoo, and so forth to keep in your car. When you see someone in need you are prepared.

Adopt a US soldier: Gatorade, Crystal Light Singles, beef jerky, beef sausage (very popular), candy, canned meats, chocolate (they don't care if it's melted), cookies, gum, mints, aspirin, cough drops, dental floss, disposable razors, Kleenex, Neosporin, mouthwash (without alcohol), lip balm, batteries, pens, your local newspapers/comics (great way to recycle all those extra newspapers)

Natural disaster victims: water, personal hygiene items, baby wipes, diapers, nonperishable food items, feminine products, toilet paper, paper towels, cleaning supplies, pet food, cough drops

We've also collected groceries at home and waited until we heard of a specific need. I've given bags of groceries to complete strangers.

I'd like to share a story with you now, one that has stayed with me for several years and touched me to the core. Watching the news one day I learned that a local family lost their teenage son in a car accident. As it turned out, just one short week earlier the mother of this child had attended a couponing workshop, a fact I never would have known had a relative not reached out. Although I didn't teach that workshop, as soon as I heard about this tragedy my heart ached for this precious family.

Over the next few weeks I developed a relationship with the mother through email. We had never met, and I have never been forced to walk in her shoes, but I understand grief. I also understand what it feels like to lose someone you love and have the grief wash over you in never-ending waves. One after another, people try to lift your spirits, yet at the same time they say things that create great expectations. *How are you doing?* Such a simple question but one that feels so loaded when you are overwhelmed with grief. It's as though they think you *should* be better by now.

Since I understood not to ask these kinds of questions or make these kinds of comments, the two of us were able to be real with each other without unrealistic expectations. I remember telling her if she wanted to call me and scream her head off or cry or get angry she could. Whatever she wanted, her pain was safe with me.

Then, a month or so later I received a phone call from an individual who wanted to act as a secret Santa for this family. This person offered to send me a check for $500 and wanted me to shop for them. I jumped at the chance. Not only would I have a chance to help the woman who had become my friend, but I would also finally get to meet her family.

When I took the groceries to their house I was scared. I didn't know what to expect. I couldn't even begin to measure the grief they were experiencing. All I had to offer was groceries, and it felt like I was carting a single bucket of water to a whale that lay beached on the sand. Yes, it needs the water to live, but what good does one bucket do?

Imagine my surprise when we pulled into the driveway and were treated like old friends. It felt like we had known each other forever, although until that night our only contact had been through email. They invited us into their home as we all carried the bags inside.

I watched with tears as these parents who had just lost their son opened bag after bag of groceries and excitedly told me how everything I bought was their favorite. "How did you know?" they asked me. I didn't. What I did know, however, was what God told me in that moment: *This is what it looks like to be my hands and feet. And this is what it looks like to minister to hurting souls; I always feed my sheep first.*

I stood back in wonder because I couldn't believe they were smiling, that something as simple as a bag of groceries could make them feel cared for. But it's a basic need. No matter what we are going through we still have to eat. From that moment I realized how powerful giving could be.

Deep, Deep Down in Their Hearts

Another facet of giving that is important to me is that I want it to be a legacy I offer to my children. If I am waiting for this world to teach my children to give, then I am setting myself up for a huge disappointment. I want to instill in them the virtues of empathy, selflessness, and kindness toward others that I learned from my daddy.

Through coupons they have experienced delayed gratification, a rarity in our society. They realize that just because we come home from the store one week without Teddy Grahams, it doesn't mean that Mommy doesn't love them. I will be happy to buy them Teddy Grahams once they are on sale and I have a coupon for them. So far this practice hasn't scarred them for life and DCS has not come knocking at my door. Instead my kids know that their favorite treats will eventually arrive in the pantry and they look forward to picking out items to donate each time we go to the grocery store. It's not always big, but it's something.

The first thing I noticed was that my children began to talk about giving. They wanted to know what we were buying to donate and they started asking about the people these items would go to. They started to look beyond themselves and consider the needs of others. I've watched their hearts become tender to those less fortunate and have seen a lifestyle of purposeful giving take root and grow.

Want to know something that will fill your heart and rip it out at the same time? Watching your child reach deep into their own piggy bank to give. It's one thing to pick out donation items when Mommy is footing the bill. It's something entirely different when you can see this transformation take root and spill over into every area of their lives.

My sweet daughter is especially sensitive to the needs of others. A dear friend of mine has endured a very difficult season in her life. Her young son was diagnosed with brain cancer several years ago. After surgery, chemo, and radiation he is cancer free and has been for several years. Morgan, my daughter, was only five when I told her about my friend's son and that we needed to make sure to include him in our prayers. We had a postcard with his picture tacked up on the fridge as a constant reminder.

Keep in mind that Morgan had never met or even talked to this boy, yet several years ago she sat down, drew him a picture, filled the envelope full of change, and asked if I would send it to him. All on her own and all without a single word from me. More recently this child lost the hearing in one of his ears and I told my kids again that he needed our prayers. Again, Morgan, following her sweet little heart, drew a picture of him sitting in the palm of Jesus's hand. She had just received a crisp new twenty-dollar bill from her grandparents in the mail that day. Before we knew what she was doing she slipped her money into the letter she was sending to my friend's son. She told me, "Mommy, I like to get toys and buy stuff, but that good feeling goes away really fast. Then my new toy isn't so new anymore and it's not fun. When I give, that good feeling in my heart doesn't go away. It feels so much better."

My child has developed a heart of giving and I couldn't feel more blessed. Both of my children have become cheerful givers at the ages of six and nine, and they have learned the truth in God's Word that it is better to give than to receive. As a result I have seen that principle spill over into their relationship with each other. Instead of always arguing over wanting to play with the same toy, sometimes they argue because each of them wants the other to go first. I've watched my six-year-old son, Caleb, become more aware of those in need. I see him watching his sister's lead. How it must make God's heart swell with joy when we reach out to our brothers and sisters in Christ!

My daughter was diagnosed with type 1 diabetes two months after she turned three. Although I would take it away from her in a minute if I could, I am thankful that diabetes is manageable. No, it's not fun for her to have to check her blood sugar ten times a day, wear an insulin pump, or count the carbs in every bite of food that she eats. Nonetheless, there is a reason. I once heard a message that I have carried with me the past couple of years. If God could do what he wanted to in my life any other way than what I am currently facing, he would have. If I'm going through it, he has a plan and a purpose. This is the perspective I choose to live by.

There are times when Caleb has to make sacrifices for Morgan because of her diabetes. If we need to treat low blood sugar, she needs a juice box immediately. Just in case she gets low, I have to make sure we always have some on hand in her room, my purse, the car, and her backpack. There are times when we don't have an extra juice box to give Caleb and have to tell him no. Years ago a huge fit would follow that response. But now Caleb always wants to make sure that Morgan has been taken care of before he even asks for juice for himself.

I know he's only six; however, he could easily internalize his not getting juice as us favoring his sister over him. Instead, he has developed compassion for her. Instead of just looking at his want, he has recently become very sensitive to her health. Morgan is also allergic to nuts. Caleb has taken it upon himself to be the "nut police." At home, church, homeschool group, and elsewhere he's always looking out for her, making sure that there are no nuts anywhere nearby. I see that his little heart has changed from thinking "I want my juice *now*!" to "If there is any left when Sissy feels better, can I have some?"

Are my children perfect? Well yes, of course they are! Totally kidding; of course not. They still get in trouble, pitch a fit from time to time, and will totally forget anything that resembles giving to one another. I tell you this because I want you to understand that I don't have strange robot children. The difference I see is in their hearts. God has used our family's mission of giving to shape their hearts to be more like him. In all humility, most of the time I don't have a clue what I'm doing.

Beyond my own family, there are thousands of people who have taken this exact message you have in your hands right now and made it their family's mission. According to God's rules of seedtime and harvest, there will be a harvest in your own family from the seeds that you plant in the lives of others. It doesn't stop there. It's a beautiful gift that goes from your heart into someone else's hand, then from their hand into their hearts. Then, the person who was once in need begins to see their life transform. As a result, they begin to water that seed you planted. Before you know it, they begin to stock their food pantry and purchase items for families in need.

We ended chapter 7 talking about my friend Jamie, who so unselfishly invested in the life of her needy friend each week. Do you know what that friend is doing now? Jamie taught her how to coupon, and now she is using the skills she learned to provide for her extended family. Who knows what the harvest of the seed she is planting will be? You may not think your impact makes a difference; the truth is you'll never know how great your impact is. You'll never know all the people who were touched by your decision to give. You'll never know how many lives will be transformed, how many people will ultimately see the hands and feet of Christ touching their lives.

All from a little slip of paper called a coupon. Miracles birthed out of a season of hardship and financial difficulty in your own life. God truly makes all things beautiful in his time. If there is one message I hope you hold on to, it's this: couponing is not just about getting a deal, it's about making a difference.

This is my story; God only knows what yours will be. All he needs is a willing vessel. It doesn't have to be a perfect or strong vessel, just one willing to be poured into. That's all he asks; all of the other stuff God has covered. Trust me, I've lived it. Weak vessels can be influenced and moved by outside forces. Weak vessels have learned to hear their Father's voice because he is the one who has lifted their lives out of the pit. No matter the pain, no matter the circumstance, God is more than able to transform and give beauty for ashes. This book is a testimony of his faithfulness.

Now it's your turn. Make a difference, give big, love bigger, and experience the transforming power of God's hand moving through your life to touch others.

ACTION STEP

Look to the future.

As we close out this final chapter, I hope that this ending can be a new beginning for you. I challenge you to open your heart to an invitation to give, to bless others with your future abundance. If you are struggling right now, then the most important first step is to focus on digging yourself out of that pit. I've been in that lonely, desperate place with you, so I know that is absolutely your first calling. But once you have gained a foothold on solid ground, I ask you to glance around you. Widen your gaze to those who are still struggling daily to somehow get food on the table or scrape together enough for diapers or toiletries. Ask yourself what you can do, then go out and do it. This transformation from needing to providing is one of the most life-changing, empowering experiences you could ever hope to undergo.

May God bless you in this endeavor.

> No, this is the kind of fasting I want:
> Free those who are wrongly imprisoned;
>   lighten the burden of those who work for you.
> Let the oppressed go free,
>   and remove the chains that bind people.
> Share your food with the hungry,
>   and give shelter to the homeless.
> Give clothes to those who need them,
>   and do not hide from relatives who need your help.

Then your salvation will come like the dawn,
    and your wounds will quickly heal.
Your godliness will lead you forward,
    and the glory of the Lord will protect you from behind.
Then when you call, the Lord will answer.
    "Yes, I am here," he will quickly reply.

Remove the heavy yoke of oppression.
    Stop pointing your finger and spreading vicious rumors!
Feed the hungry,
    and help those in trouble.
Then your light will shine out from the darkness,
    and the darkness around you will be as bright as noon.
The Lord will guide you continually,
    giving you water when you are dry
    and restoring your strength.
You will be like a well-watered garden,
    like an ever-flowing spring.

                                       Isaiah 58:6–11

Appendix A

Taking Stock of Your Pantry

Condiments	Quantity on Hand	Need (12 weeks)
BBQ sauce		
Honey mustard		
Jelly		
Ketchup		
Mayo		
Mustard		
Pickles		
Salad dressings		

Baking Essentials	Quantity on Hand	Need (12 weeks)
Baking powder		
Baking soda		

Chocolate chips		
Cooking oils (sprays, olive, and canola)		
Cornmeal		
Flour		
Nuts (walnuts, pecan, almonds)		
Spices		
Sugar (powdered, granulated, brown)		
Syrup		
Vanilla extract		

Snacks	Quantity on Hand	Need (12 weeks)
Breakfast bars		
Chips		
Crackers		
Granola bars		
Peanut butter		
Popcorn		
Pretzels		

Drinks	Quantity on Hand	Need (12 weeks)
Coffee		
Fruit juice		
Soda		
Tea		
Vegetable juice		
Water		

Rice/Pasta/Beans	Quantity on Hand	Need (12 weeks)
Beans (red, chili, green, pinto)		
Box sides (potatoes, rice, mac and cheese, etc.)		
Broths (chicken, beef, etc.)		
Pasta (spaghetti, angel hair, elbow macaroni, bow-tie, etc.)		
Pasta sauce		
Rice (white, yellow, brown)		

Household Items	Quantity on Hand	Need (12 weeks)
Aluminum foil, plastic wrap, wax paper, etc.		
Batteries		
Bleach		
Candles		
Cleaner (floor and glass)		
Dishwashing soap (liquid, tablets, gel, etc.)		
Freezer bags		
Furniture polish (wipes and sprays)		
Garbage bags		
Laundry detergent		
Paper plates		
Paper towels		
Sandwich bags		
Scents (plug-ins, refills, etc.)		
Stain remover		
Tissues		
Toilet paper		

Personal List	Quantity on Hand	Need (12 weeks)
Baby wipes		
Body wash (men's and women's)		
Deodorant		
Diapers		
Mouthwash		
Razors/shavers		
Shaving cream		
Soap (hand and bar)		
Toothbrush		
Toothpaste		

Feminine Supplies	Quantity on Hand	Need (12 weeks)
Hygiene wipes		
Pads		
Tampons		

Medicine	Quantity on Hand	Need (12 weeks)
Cold/flu remedy		
Fever reducer		
Headache/aches and pains		
Sinus		
Stomach		

Children's Medicine	Quantity on Hand	Need (12 weeks)
Children's pain reliever		

Appendix B

Stockpiling List

Canned/Boxed Items	Good Price	Stockpile Price
Cake mix		
Canned condensed soup		
Canned soup		
Canned veggies		
Cereal		
Oatmeal		
Pasta		
Rice		

Staples	Good Price	Stockpile Price
Bread		
Eggs		
Flour		
Juice		

Milk		
Sugar		

Household Items	Good Price	Stockpile Price
Cleaning supplies		
Laundry detergent		
Paper plates		
Paper towels		
Storage bags		
Toilet paper		

Personal Care Items	Good Price	Stockpile Price
Shampoo/Conditioner		
Toothpaste		

Baby Items	Good Price	Stockpile Price
Baby food		
Diapers		
Wipes		

Frozen	Good Price	Stockpile Price
Family frozen dinners		
Frozen veggies		
Single frozen dinners		

Beverages	Good Price	Stockpile Price
12-pack		
2-liters		
Bottled water		
Crystal Light		

Condiments & Snacks	Good Price	Stockpile Price
Bagged cookies		
Fruit snacks		
Granola bars		
Ketchup		
Mustard		
Other Sauces		
Peanut butter		
Pickles		
Popcorn		
Salad dressing/BBQ sauce		
Yogurt (4 pk.)		

Appendix C

Learning the Lingo

Types of Coupons

blinkie. A small box that dispenses coupons in a store, placed near the product.

CAT or Catalina. Coupon that prints at the register after your purchase is complete.

e-coupon. Electronic coupon added to store loyalty card, subtracted from order at checkout.

insert. Coupons in Sunday newspaper: Smart Source (SS), Proctor & Gamble (PG), and Red Plum (RP).

IP or printable. Internet printed coupon.

peelie. A coupon in the form of a sticker that has to be peeled off to redeem.

PG or P&G. Proctor & Gamble Sunday insert.

RP. Red Plum insert in the Sunday newspaper.

SS. Smart Source booklet, blinkie, or printable coupon issued through News Marketing America.

tear pad. Pad of coupons found on a store display, shelf, or freezer door.

wine tag, ring tag, or hang tag. A coupon hanging from the neck of a product.

Types of Sales and Coupons

B1G1 or BOGO. Buy one, get one free.

B1G1F. Buy one, get one free.

B2G1. Buy two, get one free.

$/$$. A dollar amount off a total dollar amount.

Specific Store Lingo

FLIP. Food Lion internet printable.

HIPS. Harvey's internet printable.

Drugstore Lingo

CVS. Drugstore with its own rewards/coupon saving system.

ECB. Extra Care Bucks; coincide with Extra Care Card at CVS.

IVC. Instant Value Coupon (Walgreens and CVS).

RR. Register Reward printed at the end of a transaction at Walgreens in the form of a Catalina.

SCR. Single Check Rebate issued in the form of one check at Rite Aid for various rebate offers.

+UP. Rite Aid Plus Up Reward.

WAG. Walgreens.

Coupon Terms

CRT. Cash register tape.

DND. Do not double.

double coupon. A coupon that a grocery store doubles in value depending on policy.

FAR. Free after rebate.

MFR, MQ, or Manny Q. Manufacturer coupon.

MIR. Mail-in rebate.

MM. Money maker.

NED. No expiration date.

OOP. Out of pocket.

OOS. Out of stock.

overage. This applies when the cost of an item is less than the coupon value.

OYNO. On your next order.

rebate. Mail-in offer by a manufacturer or store that issues a refund based on predetermined criteria.

RC or rain check. A piece of paper that guarantees the sale price of an out-of-stock item.

WSL. While supplies last.

WYB. When you buy.

YMMV. Your mileage may vary.

Appendix D

Internet Printable Coupons

Things to Know

- To avoid filling up your inbox, try creating an email account to use specifically for coupon-related information.
- When you are searching for internet printables on manufacturer's websites, always look for words like promotion, savings, coupons, register, login, and so on.
- Most companies will ask you to register with their website before giving you access to current offers.

What happens when the coupon doesn't print?

- First, try downloading the tool bar for the printing software, as your computer may not have it.
- Most sites will only allow two prints of a specific coupon per computer per month.
- Most printables only allow a certain number of prints before they become unavailable. To avoid missing out on your favorites,

make a habit of checking the coupon sites at the first of the month when they reset.

- If you are receiving continual messages to download the printer software but you know you've already downloaded it, head to the Time 2 $ave blog and look for the subhead "Helpful Tips."

Appendix E

Sample Binder Categories

Baby Items

Breakfast & Baking Items

Canned & Boxed Items

Cleaning Items

Drinks & Breads

Frozen Foods

Medicine

Paper Items

Personal Items

Pets

Refrigerated Foods

Sauces & Snacks

Scented Products

Appendix F

Couponing Questions to Ask at the Store

What is your store's coupon policy?

Where can I find a copy of the policy for future reference? Online? In the store?

Do you double or triple coupons? *If yes, then:*

Is there a limit on the number of total coupons that you double or triple?

Do you limit the number of like coupons you double?

Do you offer special sales or discounts at certain times? (e.g., senior day or double coupons after 6 p.m.)

What day does your circular come out? Can I find it in the paper? Online? In the store?

If the circular is available in the store, what day can I get a copy?

What day does your new sale cycle start?

What is your BOGO policy?

Do you accept competitor coupons? *If yes, then:*

Who do you consider to be a competitor?

Is there a limit on the number of competitor coupons that can be used per transaction?

Do you accept $/$$ coupons from other stores? (e.g., $2 off $5 of produce)

Will you substitute your house brand for a competitor's house brand? (e.g., $1 off Food Lion eggs = $1 off Publix eggs)

Will you match sale prices from other stores?

Is there a limit on how many coupons you can use per transaction?

Is there a limit on how many sale items that can be purchased per transaction?

Special sales such as 10/$10: Do I have to purchase ten to get the $1 per item price, or can I just purchase one?

Do you have any coupons today?

Appendix G

Tips on Storage
While Stockpiling

- It is important to keep an eye on your expiration dates. By rotating your stock each time you go to the store, you can pull the oldest product to the front of your shelves while placing the newer items to the back. This helps you keep track of what you have and avoid allowing items to expire before you have a chance to use them.

- Always have a good idea of where you want to store your stockpile before your start bringing it home from the store. Keep in mind that your daughter's bedroom is not the best place to start!

- A dry basement is a great place to store your stockpile. Just make sure that the area is weatherproof and does not leak.

- The same goes for the garage. All you need are a few sets of sturdy shelves and you are ready to go.

- If you are able to stock up on dry goods like flour, sugar, and rice, consider buying plastic bins or tubs to store them. This will help keep the food fresh and protect it from all the little critters that would love to steal a bite or two.

- Don't stockpile something you won't use just because it is on sale. If you know that your family won't use a specific item, either donate it right away or don't buy it in the first place.

- Take the time to go through your stockpile periodically and find items to donate. After all, new sales come around every week and there will always be someone who could really benefit from an item that is doing nothing more than taking up space on your shelf.

Appendix H

The Ten-Minute Trick

I've found that mealtime is much less daunting if I take a few minutes to prepare ahead of time. By cooking and freezing quantities of ground beef, ground turkey, or chicken breast to have on hand, you'll cut down your meal preparation time significantly. I call it the "The Ten-Minute Trick." Grab a ziplock bag of precooked meat or poultry from the freezer, pop it in the microwave for a minute to thaw, and then add to your favorite recipe.

Here's how!

Chicken Breast

Grill multiple packages of boneless skinless chicken breast. Once cooled, divide into freezer bags and press to get all of the air out. Seal, and place flat in freezer. You may slice the cooked, cooled breasts before freezing, if you choose.

Alternately, fill your Crock-Pot two-thirds full with thawed bone-in or boneless chicken breasts. Add salt, pepper, about four cups of chicken broth, and enough water to cover chicken completely. Cook seven to eight hours on low. Remove breasts and allow to cool, then divide into family-sized servings in freezer bags. Add a little broth to each bag to keep the chicken from drying out, and reserve the remainder (see below). Flatten freezer bag gently to get all of the air out, seal, and place flat in the freezer. Store the remainder of the broth as described below.

Chicken Broth

Strain remainder of chicken broth from Crock-Pot through a fine sieve placed over a large bowl. (You can also strain it through a colander with a paper towel placed in it.) Divide strained broth into freezer bags; 2 cups of broth is 16 oz. (a little more than a can of broth). Press bags slowly and carefully to get all of the air out, seal, and place flat in freezer. You can use broth in all kinds of recipes. By freezing it you won't have to buy as much.

Ground Beef or Ground Turkey

Place ground beef or turkey into a tall stockpot and break apart with spoon. I usually brown about five pounds at a time. Turn burner on low and set a timer for twenty minutes. When timer beeps, stir ground beef, then set timer again. You will follow the same pattern for about an hour or until ground beef or turkey is no longer pink. Pour browned ground beef or turkey into colander, rinse, and strain excess grease. Cool, and then divide into freezer bags. Your serving size will depend on your family. Generally a pound of beef will serve a family. I try to stretch mine and freeze in batches of ¾ pound. Press freezer bags gently to remove air, seal, and then place flat in freezer.

Appendix I

Freezer Help

Freezes Well

Avocados	Flavored coffee creamer	Pasta, cooked
Berries	Goat cheese	Poultry, cooked and off the bone
Bread	Green onions	Shredded cheese
Butter	Guacamole	Strawberries, flash-frozen
Cheese singles	Herbs—basil, cilantro, dill, mint, oregano, parsley, sage, thyme, and rosemary	Tortillas
Cookies	Hot dogs	Yeast
Croutons	Margarine, sticks and tubs	Yogurt tubes
Egg Beaters	Orange juice	

Freezes Okay

Bananas	Cream cheese	Milk
Block cheese	Lemons, whole	Onions and green peppers, chopped and flash-frozen

186

Cottage cheese	Lunchmeat	Pillsbury Crescents and Flaky Layers
Ricotta cheese	Soy milk	Eggs, cracked

Do Not Freeze

Apples, whole or chopped/sliced	Gelatin	Melon
Cornstarch	Mayonnaise	Meringue

Kasey Knight Trenum hosts Time 2 $ave / Time 2 Give, a national coupon and financial literacy organization (www.time2saveworkshops. com), and conducts Time 2 $ave workshops frequently. Audiences love her humor and authentic Southern charm. Her weekly column can be read in Scripps newspapers nationwide, and her work has been featured in *Parade* magazine and *All You* magazine. Kasey has been interviewed on NPR's *All Things Considered* and HLN's *Making It in America*. She has a personal passion for seeing women, men, and families find financial freedom, be empowered to improve their lives, and become purposeful givers. She lives with her husband and children in Cleveland, Tennessee.

CONNECT WITH

Kasey Knight Trenum